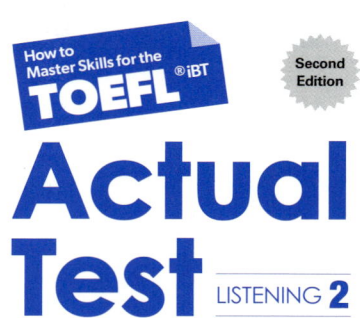

Actual Test LISTENING 2

Publisher Kyudo Chung
Editor Inpyo Hong
Authors Michael A. Putlack, Stephen Poirier, Will Link
Proofreader Michael A. Putlack
Designers Minji Kim, Hyounju Yoon

First Published in March 2008 By Darakwon, Inc.
Second edition first published in September 2025 by Darakwon, Inc.
Darakwon Bldg., 211, Munbal-ro, Paju-si, Gyeonggi-do 10881
Republic of Korea
Tel: 02-736-2031 (Ext. 250)
Fax: 02-732-2037

Copyright © 2008 Darakwon, 2025 Darakwon

All rights reserved. No part of this publication may be reproduced, stored in a retrieval system, or transmitted in any form or by any means, electronic, mechanical, photocopying or otherwise, without the prior consent of the copyright owner. Refund after purchase is possible only according to the company regulations. Contact the above telephone number for any inquiries. Consumer damages caused by loss, damage, etc. can be compensated according to the consumer dispute resolution standards announced by the Korea Fair Trade Commission. An incorrectly collated book will be exchanged.

ISBN 978-89-277-8107-3 14740
978-89-277-8105-9 14740 (set)

www.darakwon.co.kr

Photo Credits
Shutterstock.com

Components Main Book / Answer Key / Free MP3 Downloads
7 6 5 4 3 2 1   25 26 27 28 29

Table of Contents

Actual Test 01 009

Actual Test 02 027

Actual Test 03 045

Actual Test 04 063

Actual Test 05 081

Actual Test 06 099

Actual Test 07 117

Actual Test 08 135

INTRODUCTION

1 Information on the TOEFL® iBT

A The Format of the TOEFL® iBT

Section	Number of Questions or Tasks	Timing	Score

Reading	**20 Questions**
	• 2 reading passages
	  – with 10 questions per passage
	  – approximately 700 words long each
		35 Minutes	30 Points

Listening	**28 Questions**
	• 2 conversations
	  – 5 questions per conversation
	  – 3 minutes each
	• 3 lectures
	  – 6 questions per lecture
	  – 3-5 minutes each
		36 Minutes	30 Points

Speaking	**4 Tasks**
	• 1 independent speaking task
	  – 1 personal choice/opinion/experience
	  – preparation: 15 sec. / response: 45 sec.
	• 2 integrated speaking tasks: Read-Listen-Speak
	  – 1 campus situation topic
	    reading: 75-100 words (45 sec.)
	    conversation: 150-180 words (60-80 sec.)
	  – 1 academic course topic
	    reading: 75-100 words (50 sec.)
	    lecture: 150-220 words (60-120 sec.)
	  – preparation: 30 sec. / response: 60 sec.
	• 1 integrated speaking task: Listen-Speak
	  – 1 academic course topic
	    lecture: 230-280 words (90-120 sec.)
	  – preparation: 20 sec. / response: 60 sec.
		17 Minutes	30 Points

Writing	**2 Tasks**
	• 1 integrated writing task: Read-Listen-Write
	  – reading: 230-300 words (3 min.)
	  – lecture: 230-300 words (2 min.)
	  – a summary of 150-225 words (20 min.)
	• 1 academic discussion task
	  – a minimum 100-word essay (10 min.)
		30 Minutes	30 Points

B What Is New about the TOEFL® iBT?

- The TOEFL® iBT is delivered through the Internet in secure test centers around the world at the same time.
- It tests all four language skills and is taken in the order of Reading, Listening, Speaking, and Writing.
- The test is about 2 hours long, and all of the four test sections will be completed in one day.
- Note taking is allowed throughout the entire test, including the Reading section. At the end of the test, all notes are collected and destroyed at the test center.
- In the Listening section, one lecture may be spoken with a British or Australian accent.
- There are integrated tasks requiring test takers to combine more than one language skill in the Speaking and Writing sections.
- In the Speaking section, test takers wear headphones and speak into a microphone when they respond. The responses are recorded and transmitted to ETS's Online Scoring Network.
- In the Writing section, test takers must type their responses. Handwriting is not possible.
- Test scores will be reported online. Test takers can see their scores online 4-8 business days after the test and can also receive a copy of their score report by mail.

2 Information on the Listening Section

The Listening section of the TOEFL® iBT measures test takers' ability to understand spoken English in English-speaking colleges and universities. This section has 2 conversations that are 12-25 exchanges (about 3 minutes) long and 3 lectures that are 500-800 words (3-5 minutes) long. Each conversation is followed by 5 questions and each lecture by 6 questions. Therefore, test takers have to answer 28 questions in total. The time allotted to the Listening section is 36 minutes, including the time spent listening to the conversations and lectures and answering the questions.

A Types of Listening Conversations and Lectures

- Conversations
  - Between a student and a professor or a teaching assistant during office hours
  - Between a student with a person related to school services such as a librarian, a housing director, a bookstore employee, etc.

- Lectures
  - Monologue lectures delivered by a professor unilaterally
  - Interactive lectures with one or two students asking questions or making comments
    cf. One lecture may be spoken with a British or Australian accent.

B Types of Listening Questions

Type 1 Gist-Content Questions

Gist-Content questions cover the test taker's basic comprehension of the listening passage. While they are typically asked after lectures, they are sometimes asked after conversations as well. These questions check to see if the test taker has understood the gist of the passage. They focus on the passage as a whole, so it is important to recognize what the main point of the lecture is or why the two people in the conversation are having a particular discussion. The test taker should therefore be able to recognize the theme of the lecture or conversation in order to answer this question correctly. On occasion, the test taker is asked to identify two correct answers to a single question.

Type 2 Gist-Purpose Questions

Gist-Purpose questions cover the underlying theme of the passage. While they are typically asked after conversations, they are sometimes asked after lectures as well. Because these questions focus on the purpose or theme of the conversation or lecture, they begin with the word "why." They focus on the conversation or lecture as a whole, but they are not concerned with details; instead, they are concerned with why the student is speaking with the professor or employee or why the professor is covering a specific topic.

Type 3 Detail Questions

Detail questions cover the test taker's ability to understand facts and data that are mentioned in the listening passage. These questions most commonly appear after lectures; however, they also come after conversations, especially when the conversations are about academic topics. Detail questions require the test taker to listen for and remember details from the passage. The majority of these questions concern major details that are related to the main topic of the lecture or conversation rather than minor ones. However, in some cases when there is a long digression that is not clearly related to the main idea, there may be a question about the details of the digression. On occasion, the test taker is asked to identify two correct answers to a single question. These questions may also appear as charts.

Type 4 Understanding Function Questions

Understanding Function questions cover the test taker's ability to determine the underlying meaning of what has been said in the passage. This question type often involves replaying a portion of the listening passage. There are two types of these questions. Some ask the test taker to infer the meaning of a phrase or a sentence. Thus the test taker needs to determine the implication—not the literal meaning—of the sentence. Other questions ask the test taker to infer the purpose of a statement made by one of the speakers. These questions specifically ask about the intended effect of a particular statement on the listener.

Type 5 Understanding Attitude Questions

Understanding Attitude questions cover the speaker's attitude or opinion toward something. These questions may appear after both lectures and conversations. This question type often involves replaying a portion of the listening passage. There are two types of these questions. Some ask about one of the speaker's feelings concerning something. These questions may check to see whether the test taker understands how a speaker feels about a particular topic, if a speaker likes or dislikes something, or why a speaker might feel anxiety or amusement. The other category asks about one of the speaker's opinions. These questions may inquire about a speaker's degree of certainty. Others may ask what a speaker thinks or implies about a topic, person, thing, or idea.

Type 6 Understanding Organization Questions

Understanding Organization questions cover the test taker's ability to determine the overall organization of the passage. These questions almost always appear after lectures. They rarely appear after conversations. These questions require the test taker to pay attention to two factors. The first is the way that the professor has organized the lecture and how the professor presents the information to the class. The second is how individual information given in the lecture relates to the lectures as a whole. To answer these questions correctly, the test taker should focus more on the presentation and the professor's purpose in mentioning the facts rather than the facts themselves.

Type 7 Connecting Content Questions

Connecting Content questions almost exclusively appear after lectures, not after conversations. These questions measure the test taker's ability to understand how the ideas in the lecture relate to one another. These relationships may be explicitly stated, or the test taker may have to infer them from the words that are spoken. The majority of these questions concern major relationships in the passage. These questions also commonly appear in passages in which a number of different themes, ideas, objects, or individuals are being discussed.

Type 8 — Making Inference Questions

Making Inferences questions cover the test taker's ability to understand implications made in the passage and to come to a conclusion about what these implications mean. These questions appear after both conversations and lectures. These questions require the test taker to hear the information being presented and then to make conclusions about what the information means or what is going to happen as a result of that information.

How to Master Skills for the
TOEFL® iBT

Actual Test
LISTENING 2

01

TOEFL LISTENING

Listening Section Directions

This section measures your ability to understand conversations and lectures in English.

The Listening section is divided into separately timed parts. In each part, you will listen to 1 conversation and 1 or 2 lectures. You will hear each conversation or lecture only **one** time.

After each conversation and lecture, you will answer questions about it. The questions typically ask about the main idea and supporting details. Some questions ask about a speaker's purpose or attitude. Answer the questions based on what is stated or implied by the speakers.

You may take notes while you listen. You may use your notes to help you answer the questions. Your notes will not be scored.

If you need to change the volume while you listen, click on the **Volume** icon at the top of the screen.

In some questions, you will see this icon: 🎧 This means that you will hear, but not see, part of the question.

Some of the questions have special directions. These directions appear in a gray box on the screen.

Most questions are worth 1 point. If a question is worth more than 1 point, it will have special directions that indicate how many points you can receive.

A clock at the top of the screen will show you how much time is remaining. The clock will not count down while you are listening. The clock will count down only while you are answering the questions.

1 What do the speakers mainly discuss?
- Ⓐ The student's need to attend class
- Ⓑ The student's potential grade in class
- Ⓒ The student's stay in the hospital
- Ⓓ The student's absence from class

2 According to the professor, what will happen when a student misses three classes?
- Ⓐ The student will receive a warning from the teacher.
- Ⓑ The professor will call a meeting with the student.
- Ⓒ The student will be penalized on his final grade.
- Ⓓ The student will have to make up the missed work.

3 What can be inferred about the student?
- Ⓐ He is hoping for a high grade in the class.
- Ⓑ He is motivated to do well in the class.
- Ⓒ He wants the professor to give him special treatment.
- Ⓓ He feels that there is no way he can fail the class.

4 Listen again to part of the conversation. Then answer the question.
   What does the professor imply when she says this:
   - Ⓐ She remembers seeing the student in class.
   - Ⓑ She will talk to the student after class ends.
   - Ⓒ She is willing to speak to the student.
   - Ⓓ She has heard the student's name before.

5 Listen again to part of the conversation. Then answer the question.
   What does the professor mean when she says this:
   - Ⓐ She wants the student to show her the work he has done.
   - Ⓑ She would like the student to drop her course immediately.
   - Ⓒ She feels that the student will be successful in her class.
   - Ⓓ She believes the student should make up all the missed work.

Meteorology

6 What aspect of tornadoes does the professor mainly discuss?
- Ⓐ What to do if one approaches
- Ⓑ The Fujita rating scale numbers
- Ⓒ Myths people have about them
- Ⓓ Their formation and strength

7 What is the relationship between thunderstorms and tornadoes?
- Ⓐ Thunderstorms are a result of tornadoes.
- Ⓑ Tornadoes cannot form without thunderstorms.
- Ⓒ Tornadoes form from the updraft of thunderstorms.
- Ⓓ Thunderstorms always produce violent tornadoes.

8 What is the professor's attitude toward tornadoes?
- Ⓐ He is scared of them.
- Ⓑ He respects their power.
- Ⓒ He is angry that they occur.
- Ⓓ He is frustrated by them.

9 Which of the following statements have to do with tornado formation, strength, and safety?

Click in the correct box for each sentence.

	Formation	Strength	Safety
1 Warning time is essential.			
2 People must get to shelter quickly.			
3 They are rated on a scale from 0 to 5.			
4 They result from spinning updrafts in thunderstorms.			

10 Which of the following can be inferred about the professor?

Ⓐ He has been working at the school for a long time.
Ⓑ He has never been near a tornado before.
Ⓒ He is in charge of a group that studies tornadoes.
Ⓓ He is teaching first- and second-year students.

11 Listen again to part of the lecture. Then answer the question.
What does the professor imply when he says this: 🎧

Ⓐ Most of his students are from the nearby area.
Ⓑ The area the university is in gets many tornadoes.
Ⓒ Tornadoes are a big problem in many areas.
Ⓓ It is not surprising that tornadoes are a big problem.

PART 2 Conversation

TOEFL

LISTENING

01 - 03

Actual Test 01

1 Why does the student visit the student housing office?
- Ⓐ To reserve a dormitory room for the next semester
- Ⓑ To inquire about potential dormitory rooms
- Ⓒ To ask about the locations of dormitories on campus
- Ⓓ To find out where most juniors are likely to live

2 According to the man, which dormitory is popular with seniors?
- Ⓐ West Hall
- Ⓑ Henderson House
- Ⓒ Branson Hall
- Ⓓ Patterson Hall

3 What is the man's attitude toward the student?
- Ⓐ He is very cheerful.
- Ⓑ He is not forthcoming.
- Ⓒ He is too opinionated.
- Ⓓ He is somewhat nervous.

4 What does the student imply about her parents?
- Ⓐ They will not let her stay in a single.
- Ⓑ They feel she should live near campus.
- Ⓒ They are the ones who pay for her schooling.
- Ⓓ They want her to choose a room quickly.

5 Listen again to part of the conversation. Then answer the question. What does the student imply when she says this:
- Ⓐ She wants to change her dormitory.
- Ⓑ She woke up late for her class.
- Ⓒ She thinks the Quad is an ideal place to live.
- Ⓓ She does not like walking far to class.

Botany

6 What aspect of trees does the professor mainly discuss?
- Ⓐ The differences between deciduous and coniferous trees
- Ⓑ The purposes of roots, bark, and leaves
- Ⓒ The dangers of people cutting down too many trees
- Ⓓ The ways that trees benefit mankind

7 What are the major differences between deciduous and coniferous trees?
- Ⓐ Their seeds, flowers, and leaves
- Ⓑ Their seeds, cones, and bark
- Ⓒ Their roots, seeds, and leaves
- Ⓓ Their bark, seeds, and leaves

8 How does the professor organize the discussion on the structure of trees?
- Ⓐ By using different examples of trees as a focus point
- Ⓑ By examining the different scientific ways to examine trees
- Ⓒ By looking at each part of a tree and its purpose
- Ⓓ By describing the chemical processes going on in trees

9 Which statement is associated with which part of a tree?

Click in the correct box for each sentence.

	Roots	Bark	Leaves
1 A chemical reaction takes place here.			
2 This part absorbs water from the ground.			
3 The absorption of carbon dioxide and the release of oxygen occur here.			
4 This part can be used to check the history of local rainfall.			

10 What can be inferred about the Amazon Rainforest from the lecture?

Ⓐ It is in no immediate danger at the moment.
Ⓑ It is being logged, but it is being replanted.
Ⓒ It provides many important elements for the Earth.
Ⓓ It is in danger from logging companies.

11 Listen again to part of the lecture. Then answer the question.

Why does the professor say this: 🎧

Ⓐ She thinks that all logging companies are doing the right thing.
Ⓑ She feels that logging companies could do more to preserve forests.
Ⓒ She wants logging companies to stop all logging immediately.
Ⓓ She expects logging companies to pay more money for their trees.

History

12 What aspect of Europe prior to World War I does the professor discuss?
- Ⓐ The characteristics of European society
- Ⓑ The main reasons the war was so long and bloody
- Ⓒ The strengths and weaknesses of the Great Powers
- Ⓓ The roles of education and women in society

13 What did most European people have in common when World War I started?
- Ⓐ They belonged to a class-conscious society.
- Ⓑ They were enthusiastic about war.
- Ⓒ They had similar education levels.
- Ⓓ They all had the right to vote.

14 How does the professor organize the lecture?
- Ⓐ By examining each Great Power in turn
- Ⓑ By describing the main events before the war in chronological order
- Ⓒ By discussing the attitudes of the different classes toward war
- Ⓓ By looking closely at several aspects of society

15. Which statements are appropriate for the different areas of Europe on the eve of World War I?

Click in the correct box for each sentence.

	Western Europe	Eastern and Southern Europe
1 It had a highly agrarian society.		
2 Its economy was very industrialized.		
3 It had a good education system.		
4 Many of its people were illiterate.		

16. Listen again to part of the lecture. Then answer the question.
What can be inferred about the professor when she says this:
- Ⓐ She feels the law was appropriate for a time of war.
- Ⓑ She thinks the law was great for giving women the vote.
- Ⓒ She wanted women to have the right to vote immediately.
- Ⓓ She has a very strong opinion but agrees with the law.

17. Listen again to part of the lecture. Then answer the question.
What does the professor imply when she says this:
- Ⓐ Modern technology would not allow such a war.
- Ⓑ Modern society would not stand such a war.
- Ⓒ Modern men would not charge the enemy.
- Ⓓ Modern people do not have such dedication.

How to Master Skills for the TOEFL® iBT

Actual Test
LISTENING 2

02

TOEFL LISTENING

Listening Section Directions

This section measures your ability to understand conversations and lectures in English.

The Listening section is divided into separately timed parts. In each part, you will listen to 1 conversation and 1 or 2 lectures. You will hear each conversation or lecture only **one** time.

After each conversation and lecture, you will answer questions about it. The questions typically ask about the main idea and supporting details. Some questions ask about a speaker's purpose or attitude. Answer the questions based on what is stated or implied by the speakers.

You may take notes while you listen. You may use your notes to help you answer the questions. Your notes will not be scored.

If you need to change the volume while you listen, click on the **Volume** icon at the top of the screen.

In some questions, you will see this icon: 🎧 This means that you will hear, but not see, part of the question.

Some of the questions have special directions. These directions appear in a gray box on the screen.

Most questions are worth 1 point. If a question is worth more than 1 point, it will have special directions that indicate how many points you can receive.

A clock at the top of the screen will show you how much time is remaining. The clock will not count down while you are listening. The clock will count down only while you are answering the questions.

PART 1 Conversation

TOEFL
LISTENING

1 What are the speakers mainly discussing?
- Ⓐ The contrast in the earlier and later poems of the poet Keats
- Ⓑ A change in the class syllabus related to the homework assignment
- Ⓒ How to organize the homework assignment for the following week
- Ⓓ Some confusion in the student's understanding of the assignment topic

2 Why does the student visit the professor?
- Ⓐ To ask for an extension on her assignment
- Ⓑ To inquire about the class syllabus
- Ⓒ To question the grade on her homework
- Ⓓ To see if there was a change in the syllabus

3 What had a large effect on the student's assignment grade?
- Ⓐ Her paper exceeded the maximum length set by the professor.
- Ⓑ She failed to refer to her syllabus to learn about the assignment.
- Ⓒ She did not compare two of Keats's poems in the report.
- Ⓓ She did not follow the professor's in-class directions.

4 Listen again to part of the conversation. Then answer the question.
What does the student mean when she says this:
- Ⓐ She does not want to ask the professor.
- Ⓑ She does not believe the professor.
- Ⓒ She cannot believe what she is saying.
- Ⓓ She does not want to offend the professor.

5 Listen again to part of the conversation. Then answer the question.
What can be inferred about the student when she says this:
- Ⓐ She feels like she wasted her time by visiting the professor.
- Ⓑ She is determined to do well on the next assignment.
- Ⓒ She continues to be bitter about her first assignment grade.
- Ⓓ She believes the professor gave her valuable insight to use for later.

Marine Biology

6. What aspect of the jellyfish does the professor mainly discuss?
Click on 2 answers.
- Ⓐ The makeup of the jellyfish
- Ⓑ Deadly types of jellyfish
- Ⓒ Jellyfish defense mechanisms
- Ⓓ The cnidoblasts of the jellyfish

7. According to the professor, how does the jellyfish's gelatinous body form affect it?
- Ⓐ It allows the jellyfish to glide through the water quickly.
- Ⓑ It protects the jellyfish from dangerous predators.
- Ⓒ It helps guide the jellyfish through the ocean's currents.
- Ⓓ It hides the jellyfish's cnidoblasts from potential prey.

8. According to the professor, what is the main reason fatalities arise from box jellyfish stings?
- Ⓐ It travels in large numbers and inflicts severe damage.
- Ⓑ The neurotoxins in its tentacles attack the brain immediately.
- Ⓒ The victim already has a serious medical condition.
- Ⓓ The individual develops severe cramps and dies from drowning.

9 What is the professor's opinion of the Portuguese man o' war?
- Ⓐ She is concerned about its danger to humans.
- Ⓑ She is impressed by its developed nature.
- Ⓒ She is adamant about its declining numbers.
- Ⓓ She is surprised by its ability to evolve.

10 The following statements list characteristics of the box jellyfish and the Portuguese man o' war.

Click in the correct box for each sentence.

	Box Jellyfish	Portuguese Man o' War
① It is only found in the waters of Australia.		
② It consists of four different types of polyps.		
③ Its tentacles contain a toxic neurotoxin.		
④ It is commonly found off the U.S. east coast.		

11 Listen again to part of the lecture. Then answer the question.
What does the professor imply when she says this:
- Ⓐ The tentacles are not connected to the medusa.
- Ⓑ Jellyfish have more than two forms.
- Ⓒ The late stage of the jellyfish is the polyp.
- Ⓓ All jellyfish do not develop a medusa.

PART 2 Conversation

1 What are the speakers mainly discussing?
- Ⓐ The student's previous SAT and GRE scores
- Ⓑ The student's options after graduating from college
- Ⓒ The best path for securing a job in the publishing field
- Ⓓ The travel plans the student has made for the future

2 Why did the professor ask to see the student?
- Ⓐ To see if the student plans on becoming an editor or not
- Ⓑ To inquire whether or not the student signed up to take the GRE
- Ⓒ To convince the student to consider getting an advanced degree
- Ⓓ To demand that the student quit his current job and set some real goals

3 What is the student's current plan after graduating?
- Ⓐ To stick with his job and to take graduate classes part time
- Ⓑ To quit his current job and to travel around the world for a while
- Ⓒ To take the GRE and to apply to a number of graduate programs
- Ⓓ To save up some money and eventually to take a trip

4 What can be inferred about the student?
- Ⓐ He is an overachiever with clear goals set for himself.
- Ⓑ He has a lack of confidence in himself and his potential.
- Ⓒ He is overly ambitious in wanting to travel and to attend graduate school.
- Ⓓ He does not take the professor's advice seriously because of his poor record.

5 Listen again to part of the conversation. Then answer the question.
What does the student imply when he says this: 🎧
- Ⓐ He has never considered a career in publishing before.
- Ⓑ He always thought becoming an editor was beyond his reach.
- Ⓒ He has always believed the ultimate job would be an editing position.
- Ⓓ He believes his dream of being an editor will never come to fruition.

Physiology

6 What is the main topic of the lecture?
- Ⓐ The different ways in which humans can contract rabies
- Ⓑ Types of viruses that attack the human nervous system
- Ⓒ The reasons why rabies is such a deadly virus to animals
- Ⓓ The differences between the brain's sensory and motor functions

7 According to the professor, what makes rabies so deadly?
- Ⓐ The virus enters the body without being detected by the immune system.
- Ⓑ The virus is able to spread quickly throughout the body in a matter of hours.
- Ⓒ The virus attacks the bloodstream and kills off many white blood cells.
- Ⓓ The virus is present in many animals that come into contact with people.

8 The following statements list common symptoms of rabies when it attacks the sensory or motor functions of the brain.
Click in the correct box for each sentence.

	Sensory	Motor
① The victim will have difficulty walking.		
② The victim might experience seizures.		
③ The victim could have numb arms or legs.		
④ The victim may feel itchy.		

9 According to the professor, what is the goal of the rabies virus?
- Ⓐ To infect an animal's brain and ultimately to kill it
- Ⓑ To hide from the immune system as long as it can
- Ⓒ To proliferate in one animal and to move on to another
- Ⓓ To lie dormant in an animal until it is weak and vulnerable

10 How is the discussion organized?
- Ⓐ The professor discusses the various stages of rabies.
- Ⓑ The professor relates his personal experience with rabies.
- Ⓒ The professor describes rabies and then gives some examples.
- Ⓓ The professor moves forward in time in the lecture.

11 Listen again to part of the lecture. Then answer the question.
What does the professor imply when he says this: 🎧
- Ⓐ The rabies virus can be easily detected from its many symptoms.
- Ⓑ A person can have rabies for a long time and never know it.
- Ⓒ Victims of rabies do not like to talk about their symptoms.
- Ⓓ The symptoms of rabies are not as dangerous as the virus itself.

Archaeology

12 What aspect of the Great Pyramids does the professor mainly discuss?
- Ⓐ The definitive method employed to create them
- Ⓑ Three problematic theories on how they were built
- Ⓒ How local materials were essential to their longevity
- Ⓓ Why the alien theory is a far-fetched hypothesis

13 According to the professor, what is the main problem with the crane theory?
- Ⓐ There is no proof that the Egyptians ever built any wooden cranes.
- Ⓑ Timber was not long enough to reach the top of the pyramid.
- Ⓒ The Egyptians were not advanced enough to create many cranes.
- Ⓓ Egypt lacked the natural resources needed for its implementation.

14 What does the professor imply about the ramp theory?
- Ⓐ Men did not push stone blocks up the pyramids.
- Ⓑ It is almost certainly an incorrect theory.
- Ⓒ Animals were used to ferry blocks to the pyramids.
- Ⓓ No other forms of incline were used for the pyramids.

15 According to the professor, why was the switchback method problematic?
- Ⓐ It required many miles of ramps to be built.
- Ⓑ It did not allow for accurate measurement of the corners.
- Ⓒ It failed to allow enough room at the top for construction.
- Ⓓ It could not accommodate great numbers of men on the ramps.

16 The following statements list the characteristics of the crane and ramp theories of pyramid construction.

Click in the correct box for each sentence.

	Crane	Ramp
1 It had to compensate for extreme angles.		
2 It consisted of two different types.		
3 It was proposed by Herodotus.		
4 It is known that the Egyptians built these devices.		

17 Listen again to part of the lecture. Then answer the question.
What can be inferred about the professor when she says this:
- Ⓐ She hopes the student will do some independent research.
- Ⓑ She wishes that the student did not care about a theory.
- Ⓒ She wants her students to make their own judgments.
- Ⓓ She thinks there is more than enough proof and evidence.

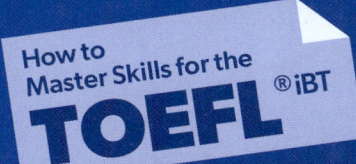

Actual Test
LISTENING 2

03

TOEFL LISTENING

Listening Section Directions

This section measures your ability to understand conversations and lectures in English.

The Listening section is divided into separately timed parts. In each part, you will listen to 1 conversation and 1 or 2 lectures. You will hear each conversation or lecture only **one** time.

After each conversation and lecture, you will answer questions about it. The questions typically ask about the main idea and supporting details. Some questions ask about a speaker's purpose or attitude. Answer the questions based on what is stated or implied by the speakers.

You may take notes while you listen. You may use your notes to help you answer the questions. Your notes will not be scored.

If you need to change the volume while you listen, click on the **Volume** icon at the top of the screen.

In some questions, you will see this icon: 🎧 This means that you will hear, but not see, part of the question.

Some of the questions have special directions. These directions appear in a gray box on the screen.

Most questions are worth 1 point. If a question is worth more than 1 point, it will have special directions that indicate how many points you can receive.

A clock at the top of the screen will show you how much time is remaining. The clock will not count down while you are listening. The clock will count down only while you are answering the questions.

PART 1 Conversation

1 Why does the student visit the professor?
- Ⓐ To discuss an issue with his class schedule
- Ⓑ To talk about a seminar that he is enrolled in
- Ⓒ To submit a paper that he completed writing
- Ⓓ To ask about her plans for the next semester

2 What can be inferred about the student?
- Ⓐ He sometimes works part time for the professor.
- Ⓑ He is considering transferring to another school.
- Ⓒ He is interested in learning about the Renaissance.
- Ⓓ He is planning to attend graduate school later.

3 What does the professor suggest that the student do?
Click on 2 answers.
- Ⓐ Take a different class that is being offered
- Ⓑ Sign up for a class at another school
- Ⓒ Register for a seminar during summer school
- Ⓓ Talk to professors in the English Department

4 What is the student's opinion of the professor?
- Ⓐ He approves of her comments on his work.
- Ⓑ He likes the way that she offers him advice.
- Ⓒ He is disappointed by her lack of assistance.
- Ⓓ He wishes she would be more helpful.

5 What will the professor probably do next?
- Ⓐ Go to her next class
- Ⓑ Attend a faculty meeting
- Ⓒ Conduct office hours
- Ⓓ Give the student an assignment

History

6 What is the lecture mainly about?
- Ⓐ The effects of European exploration in the Americas
- Ⓑ An early history of the Spanish conquistadors
- Ⓒ The agricultural exchange between the New World and Europe
- Ⓓ Reasons why Portugal and Spain explored the Americas

7 Why does the professor discuss the conquistadors?
- Ⓐ To show how they were inexperienced explorers
- Ⓑ To question their decision to slaughter natives
- Ⓒ To indicate why they were not so successful
- Ⓓ To relate the nature of their brutal exploits

8 According to the professor, what did Spain hope to gain through exploration?
- Ⓐ A better passage to the East for the spice trade
- Ⓑ Diverse agricultural products for Europe
- Ⓒ Precious metals to take back to Europe
- Ⓓ Conflict and conquest over the Aztec people

9 According to the professor, what was the most crucial result of the surplus of silver in Europe?

- Ⓐ Sugar and coffee could be developed in the New World.
- Ⓑ Trade in Eastern silks and spices increased greatly.
- Ⓒ More expeditions to the Americas could be financed.
- Ⓓ Countries' economies began to face major inflation.

10 The following statements list the contributions of Europe and the New World to each other.

Click in the correct box for each sentence.

	Europeans	People of the New World
1 Hepatitis was introduced by its people.		
2 They introduced wheat to the other.		
3 They acquainted the other with the turkey.		
4 They introduced influenza.		

11 Listen again to part of the lecture. Then answer the question.
What does the professor imply when he says this: 🎧

- Ⓐ The natives often perished from the diseases.
- Ⓑ The natives had experienced the diseases before.
- Ⓒ The natives had many remedies for the diseases.
- Ⓓ The natives were resilient people in general.

PART 2 Conversation

TOEFL
LISTENING

1 Why does the student speak with the librarian?
- Ⓐ He wants to check out some books.
- Ⓑ He needs the titles of some books.
- Ⓒ He is unable to locate some books.
- Ⓓ He forgot some books' call numbers.

2 According to the librarian, why do books sometimes get lost in the library?
- Ⓐ Students occasionally steal them.
- Ⓑ Shelf readers put them in the wrong place.
- Ⓒ The librarians change the books' locations.
- Ⓓ The call numbers are written improperly.

3 What can be inferred about the librarian?
- Ⓐ She has never failed to find a book before.
- Ⓑ She enjoys searching for books that are lost.
- Ⓒ She wants the student to look harder for the books.
- Ⓓ She is used to people asking her to find books.

4 What will the student probably do next?
- Ⓐ Go to another section of the library
- Ⓑ Start reading the book he found
- Ⓒ Verify the other book's call number
- Ⓓ Ask other students if they have a book

5 Listen again to part of the conversation. Then answer the question.
Why does the librarian say this:
- Ⓐ To say she is pleased the student found the book
- Ⓑ To indicate she is still looking for the other book
- Ⓒ To acknowledge the fact that she found the book
- Ⓓ To praise the student's ability to locate the book

PART 2 Lecture #1

6 Which characteristics of deserts does the professor mainly discuss?
Click on 2 answers.
- Ⓐ The humidity in deserts
- Ⓑ Types of sand dunes
- Ⓒ Different types of deserts
- Ⓓ Various desert formations

7 Why does the professor explain that most deserts do not have sand dunes or very much sand?
- Ⓐ To make the students understand that deserts are disappearing
- Ⓑ To get the students to see that deserts have many parts
- Ⓒ To show the students that deserts can be anywhere in the world
- Ⓓ To dispel any false notions that the students have of deserts

8 What is the relationship between wind and desert formations?
Click on 2 answers.
- Ⓐ Wind blows sand, so erosion creates rock formations.
- Ⓑ Wind must be present to create any formations in the desert.
- Ⓒ Wind blows sand into hills called dunes, which have many shapes.
- Ⓓ Water erodes rocks while wind then turns them to sand.

9 How does the professor organize the lecture?
- Ⓐ By giving examples of major world deserts and their characteristics
- Ⓑ By distinguishing between the different types of deserts
- Ⓒ By examining various characteristics of deserts in detail
- Ⓓ By discussing methods of erosion and their effects on deserts

10 What is a characteristic of a mesa?
- Ⓐ It has tall, steep canyons.
- Ⓑ It features deep water channels.
- Ⓒ It has hard central rock.
- Ⓓ It is mushroom shaped in appearance.

11 Listen again to part of the lecture. Then answer the question.
What does the professor mean when he says this: 🎧
- Ⓐ Only people with healthy hearts go to deserts because of the heat.
- Ⓑ A person must be physically and mentally ready for the heat.
- Ⓒ It is so hot in deserts that people can bake buns like in an oven.
- Ⓓ Doing research in the hot desert is the toughest thing he has ever done.

Zoology

12 What aspect of snakes does the professor mostly discuss?
- A) Where they can be found
- B) Their physical characteristics
- C) Their feeding habits
- D) Their types of venom

13 Why does the professor mention that Hawaii has no snakes?
- A) To provide an interesting fact about snakes in the United States
- B) Because she wants to move there in the future to avoid them
- C) In order to discuss why snakes are not found in some areas
- D) To let the students know it is safe to go hiking in Hawaii

14 According to the professor, how does a snake eat its food?
- A) It unhinges its jaw and swallows its prey whole.
- B) It chews its prey into tiny pieces before swallowing everything.
- C) It eats animals it kills while they are not quite dead.
- D) It kills its prey and then waits a day before eating the animal.

15 How does the professor organize the information about American snakes that she presents to the class?

Ⓐ She talks at length about both venomous and nonvenomous snakes.
Ⓑ She concentrates on the snakes found in the Southeastern states.
Ⓒ She talks mainly about the types of snakes found in different states.
Ⓓ She talks mostly about the venomous snakes and where they are.

16 What is the professor's attitude toward snakes?

Ⓐ She has no interest in them.
Ⓑ She believes they should be killed.
Ⓒ She thinks they are helpful to ecosystems.
Ⓓ She considers them dangerous.

17 Listen again to part of the lecture. Then answer the question.
What does the professor imply when she says this: 🎧

Ⓐ People should always carry a flashlight when hiking.
Ⓑ Hikers should check out every hole with a flashlight.
Ⓒ A snake could be in a hole that is dark.
Ⓓ Snakes are often more alert when people are hiking nearby.

Actual Test

LISTENING 2

04

Listening Section Directions

This section measures your ability to understand conversations and lectures in English.

The Listening section is divided into separately timed parts. In each part, you will listen to 1 conversation and 1 or 2 lectures. You will hear each conversation or lecture only **one** time.

After each conversation and lecture, you will answer questions about it. The questions typically ask about the main idea and supporting details. Some questions ask about a speaker's purpose or attitude. Answer the questions based on what is stated or implied by the speakers.

You may take notes while you listen. You may use your notes to help you answer the questions. Your notes will not be scored.

If you need to change the volume while you listen, click on the **Volume** icon at the top of the screen.

In some questions, you will see this icon: 🎧 This means that you will hear, but not see, part of the question.

Some of the questions have special directions. These directions appear in a gray box on the screen.

Most questions are worth 1 point. If a question is worth more than 1 point, it will have special directions that indicate how many points you can receive.

A clock at the top of the screen will show you how much time is remaining. The clock will not count down while you are listening. The clock will count down only while you are answering the questions.

PART 1 Conversation

1 What do the speakers mainly talk about?
- Ⓐ The Greek influence on Roman pottery
- Ⓑ Various approaches to the student's paper
- Ⓒ The student's lack of an art history education
- Ⓓ The student's upcoming class assignment

2 What kind of help does the student need from the professor?
- Ⓐ Determining the length of her paper
- Ⓑ Finding a topic for her report
- Ⓒ Knowing how many sources to use
- Ⓓ Thinking of an approach to the essay

3 What is the student probably going to do next?
- Ⓐ Visit the library
- Ⓑ Ask more questions
- Ⓒ Start writing her paper
- Ⓓ Inquire about Greek pottery influences

4 Listen again to part of the conversation. Then answer the question.
What can be inferred about the professor when he says this:

Ⓐ He does not like having students interrupt him.
Ⓑ He enjoys being visited by the student.
Ⓒ He wants the student to make an appointment next time.
Ⓓ He thinks that too few students visit his office.

5 Listen again to part of the conversation. Then answer the question.
What does the professor imply when he says this:

Ⓐ The Greeks were strong influences on Rome.
Ⓑ The library should have many books on the topic.
Ⓒ The student will get many ideas on this topic.
Ⓓ The student needs to think about the influence a lot.

History

6 What is the lecture mainly about?
- Ⓐ The way California became a state in 1850
- Ⓑ The results of the discovery of gold in California
- Ⓒ The influence of gold discoveries on migration
- Ⓓ The connection between gold and lawlessness

7 Why does the professor mention the Mexican customs of mining?
- Ⓐ To account for why individuals could take gold from government land
- Ⓑ To show that California had more Mexican influences than American ones
- Ⓒ To explain why there were many lawless people in California
- Ⓓ To prove that the Mexicans should have kept the land

8 According to the professor, what was the major negative effect of the California gold rush?
- Ⓐ The displacement of the Native Americans
- Ⓑ The influx of too many people to California
- Ⓒ The deaths from the long voyage to California
- Ⓓ The squabbling over the rights to certain claims

9 How does the professor organize the lecture?

Ⓐ By examining the major personalities involved in an event
Ⓑ By looking at the political aspects of an event
Ⓒ By comparing one event with other similar ones
Ⓓ By discussing various events and their results

10 The professor mentions several important events in the California Gold Rush. Put these events in the order they happened.
One of the answer choices will not be used.

Event 1	
Event 2	
Event 3	
Event 4	

Ⓐ President Polk announced the California gold discovery.
Ⓑ Men at Sutter's Mill discovered gold in the American River.
Ⓒ California became the thirty-first state in the Union.
Ⓓ All of the gold was discovered, and the rush ended.
Ⓔ The forty-niners descended on the California gold fields.

11 Listen again to part of the lecture. Then answer the question.
What does the professor mean when he says this:

Ⓐ Sutter spread rumors about the gold find in San Francisco.
Ⓑ People in San Francisco went out to find gold.
Ⓒ Despite Sutter's efforts, people found out about the gold.
Ⓓ The rumors about the gold find turned out to be true.

PART 1 Lecture #2

Literature

Irony

12 What is the lecture mainly about?
- Ⓐ The major differences between satire and irony
- Ⓑ Twain's literary techniques in *The Adventures of Huckleberry Finn*
- Ⓒ An exploration of the use of irony in literature
- Ⓓ The definitions of important literary terminology

13 According to the professor, what is irony?
- Ⓐ A humorous literary technique that reveals a moral problem
- Ⓑ An outcome contrary to what was actually expected by the reader
- Ⓒ An obvious symbol revealed to the reader to help with understanding
- Ⓓ The use of contradictory themes in a literary work by an author

14 Why does the professor explain the newspaper headline "Lifeguard Drowns in Pool"?
- Ⓐ To give an everyday example of literary irony
- Ⓑ To show that irony can be found virtually everywhere
- Ⓒ To note how irony is not always presented for humor
- Ⓓ To indicate it is not very difficult to create irony

15 According to the professor, why is Mark Twain's novel an example of situational irony?
- Ⓐ Huck is a funny character, yet he is still troubled.
- Ⓑ Huck fails to realize the true nature of what sin is.
- Ⓒ Huck undergoes a transformation throughout the novel.
- Ⓓ Huck ultimately helps the slave, which was unexpected.

16 The following statements list the characteristics of sarcasm and irony in literature.
Click in the correct box for each sentence.

	Sarcasm	Irony
1 It is usually more obvious.		
2 It is typically harsh in tone		
3 It is often used in satirical works.		
4 It is more ambiguous.		

17 Listen again to part of the lecture. Then answer the question.
What can be inferred from the student's response to the professor:
- Ⓐ He is excited about the professor's compliment.
- Ⓑ He is being sarcastic about the extra work.
- Ⓒ He is thankful the teacher is giving the class a break.
- Ⓓ He is disappointed the class is reading *Gulliver's Travels*.

PART 2 Conversation

TOEFL

LISTENING

1 What are the speakers mainly discussing?
- Ⓐ The value of the student's books
- Ⓑ Professor Bianconi's economics class
- Ⓒ How the student purchased his books
- Ⓓ The way the student can get his money back

2 Why does the student visit the bookstore?
- Ⓐ To complain about its refund policy
- Ⓑ To attempt to bargain with the manager
- Ⓒ To return some books he does not need
- Ⓓ To present his receipt for his books

3 According to the manager, why should the student avoid writing on the book's front cover?
- Ⓐ It means that he cannot return it.
- Ⓑ The bookstore will refuse him a refund.
- Ⓒ It makes the book worth less money.
- Ⓓ Fewer students will be willing to buy it used.

4 What is the manager's attitude toward the student?

- Ⓐ She is very businesslike in her approach.
- Ⓑ She is helpful by explaining her reasoning.
- Ⓒ She is tired of having the same books returned.
- Ⓓ She is calculating in her assessment of the books' values.

5 Listen again to part of the conversation. Then answer the question.
What can be inferred about the manager's response to the student:

- Ⓐ She thinks the student is funny.
- Ⓑ She believes the student should be careful.
- Ⓒ She wants the student to apologize.
- Ⓓ She agrees with the student.

Nutrition

6 What aspect of sugar substitutes does the professor mainly discuss?
- Ⓐ Their history and the major reasons for their development
- Ⓑ The common fallacies surrounding their everyday use
- Ⓒ The characteristics of a couple of the most popular ones
- Ⓓ The main reasons why aspartame is better than saccharin

7 According to the professor, what is the main cause of health problems for people?
- Ⓐ Because it causes cancer in lab animals, saccharin is very dangerous.
- Ⓑ It is diabetes due to the amount of natural sugar used compared to substitutes.
- Ⓒ The combination of different forms of sugar substitutes is by far the most dangerous.
- Ⓓ Overindulgence of virtually anything proves to be the greatest hazard to people.

8 According to the professor, what is a potential danger of aspartame?
- Ⓐ It can cause a higher risk of cancer in infants.
- Ⓑ It can create serious nervous system diseases.
- Ⓒ It can contribute to birth defects in unborn children.
- Ⓓ It can cause mothers to become lactose intolerant.

9. The following statements list the characteristics of the sugar substitutes saccharin and aspartame.

Click in the correct box for each sentence.

	Saccharin	Aspartame
1 It is the oldest manmade sugar substitute.		
2 The brand Equal contains this substance.		
3 It contains the amino acid phenylalanine.		
4 It is three hundred times sweeter than sugar.		

10. What can be inferred about saccharin?

- Ⓐ It was created before the substitute aspartame.
- Ⓑ It was not initially well received by consumers.
- Ⓒ It is not much stronger in flavor than natural sugar.
- Ⓓ It is cheaper to produce than other forms of sugar.

11. Listen again to part of the lecture. Then answer the question.
What does the professor imply when he says this: 🎧

- Ⓐ The FDA convinced everyone saccharin was safe.
- Ⓑ The FDA was unable to quell doubt in some people.
- Ⓒ The FDA helped people with their experiments.
- Ⓓ The FDA showed a few individuals their concern was futile.

How to Master Skills for the TOEFL® iBT

Actual Test
LISTENING 2

05

TOEFL LISTENING

Listening Section Directions

This section measures your ability to understand conversations and lectures in English.

The Listening section is divided into separately timed parts. In each part, you will listen to 1 conversation and 1 or 2 lectures. You will hear each conversation or lecture only **one** time.

After each conversation and lecture, you will answer questions about it. The questions typically ask about the main idea and supporting details. Some questions ask about a speaker's purpose or attitude. Answer the questions based on what is stated or implied by the speakers.

You may take notes while you listen. You may use your notes to help you answer the questions. Your notes will not be scored.

If you need to change the volume while you listen, click on the **Volume** icon at the top of the screen.

In some questions, you will see this icon: 🎧 This means that you will hear, but not see, part of the question.

Some of the questions have special directions. These directions appear in a gray box on the screen.

Most questions are worth 1 point. If a question is worth more than 1 point, it will have special directions that indicate how many points you can receive.

A clock at the top of the screen will show you how much time is remaining. The clock will not count down while you are listening. The clock will count down only while you are answering the questions.

PART 1 Conversation

1 What is the student's problem?
- Ⓐ She missed the special event for clubs.
- Ⓑ She does not have time to join a club.
- Ⓒ The club she wants does not exist.
- Ⓓ It is not possible to join clubs now.

2 According to the man, what problem did the cycling club encounter in the past? Click on 2 answers.
- Ⓐ There was too much wind.
- Ⓑ Temperatures were very cold.
- Ⓒ The weather was very stormy.
- Ⓓ It was too hot to go cycling.

3 What is the man's opinion of starting a new club?
- Ⓐ It is not very difficult to do.
- Ⓑ It requires some hard work.
- Ⓒ It can be highly time consuming.
- Ⓓ It costs a lot of money to do.

4 What will the student probably do next?
- Ⓐ Continue speaking with the man
- Ⓑ Visit her friend in the dormitory
- Ⓒ Attend her next class
- Ⓓ Find a course to go cycling

5 Listen again to part of the conversation. Then answer the question.
What is the purpose of the man's response: 🎧
- Ⓐ To agree with the student's comment
- Ⓑ To give an additional description
- Ⓒ To respond to an inquiry
- Ⓓ To provide some encouragement

History

6 What aspect of the American Revolution does the professor mainly discuss?
- Ⓐ The grievances of the American colonists toward the British
- Ⓑ The British system of taxation in the American colonies
- Ⓒ The presence of British troops placed in American homes
- Ⓓ The desires of the American colonists to be free of British rule

7 Why did the British impose a harsh system of taxation on the American colonies?
- Ⓐ To help the East India Company get out of debt
- Ⓑ To raise money for the maintenance of the colonies
- Ⓒ To help pay for the debt of the Seven Years' War
- Ⓓ To show the Americans that Britain was in charge

8 How does the professor organize the information in the lecture?
- Ⓐ By looking at some famous people of the colonial American era
- Ⓑ By discussing each colony and its problems with the British
- Ⓒ By showing how the Americans prepared to resist the British
- Ⓓ By examining the individual British acts and their effects

9 Which of the statements is associated with the British acts passed prior to the American Revolution?

Click in the correct box for each sentence.

	Tea Act	Intolerable Acts
1 Included the Quartering Act		
2 Resulted in colonists disposing of some ships' cargo		
3 Failed to make money for a British company		
4 Happened over a period of several years		

10 Listen again to part of the lecture. Then answer the question.
What does the professor imply when he says this:

- Ⓐ The colonists killed many of the tax collectors.
- Ⓑ Very little money was actually collected.
- Ⓒ The colonists paid the tax but did not like it.
- Ⓓ The tax collectors fought the colonists.

11 Listen again to part of the lecture. Then answer the question.
Why does the professor say this:

- Ⓐ To mention that Americans were forced to buy the East India tea
- Ⓑ To indicate that Americans refused to buy or drink tea
- Ⓒ To state that the East India Company went bankrupt
- Ⓓ To declare that no one was allowed to sell tea in America

PART 2 Conversation

TOEFL

LISTENING

1 Why does the student visit the professor?
- Ⓐ To complain about the cost of her books
- Ⓑ To ask about one of the course requirements
- Ⓒ To request some tips on how to read quickly
- Ⓓ To discuss her experiences from high school

2 According to the professor, what happened to other students who had the same concern as the female student?
- Ⓐ They mostly failed his class.
- Ⓑ They always did better than the others.
- Ⓒ They all did rather well in the class.
- Ⓓ They mostly just dropped his class.

3 What does the professor imply about the student's high school?
- Ⓐ It was not one of the country's elite schools.
- Ⓑ It was not as rigorous as the student's college.
- Ⓒ It helped prepare the student for college life.
- Ⓓ Its teachers should have taught the student more.

4. Listen again to part of the conversation. Then answer the question.
   What does the student mean when she says this:
   Ⓐ She knows she cannot cope with the workload.
   Ⓑ She believes she will complete all the work.
   Ⓒ She feels that she needs to drop the class.
   Ⓓ She is not sure if she can handle the class.

5. Listen again to part of the conversation. Then answer the question.
   What is the purpose of the professor's response:
   Ⓐ He is pleased with the student's comment.
   Ⓑ He is warning the student to try harder.
   Ⓒ He thinks the student should change her attitude.
   Ⓓ He wants the student to continue in his class.

Zoology

6 What aspect of eyes does the professor mainly discuss?
- Ⓐ How animal eyes are similar to human eyes
- Ⓑ The types and purposes of animals' eyes
- Ⓒ Colorblindness in humans and animals
- Ⓓ Poor eyesight in some animals

7 Why does the professor mention worms?
- Ⓐ To compare their eyes with those of birds
- Ⓑ To point out that they have directional eyes
- Ⓒ To claim that they are likely colorblind
- Ⓓ To say that their eyes are surprisingly advanced

8 According to the professor, what is the main difficulty in studying animal eyes and vision?
- Ⓐ They are difficult to control in test situations.
- Ⓑ Some animals have poor vision and easily attack.
- Ⓒ People cannot communicate with animals.
- Ⓓ People do not know how they form images.

9. According to the professor, what can the eyes of baboons do?
   Click on 2 answers.
   - (A) Become brighter than normal
   - (B) See in a 287-degree arc
   - (C) Increase in size
   - (D) See in the infrared spectrum

10. Listen again to part of the lecture. Then answer the question.
    What does the professor mean when she says this:
    - (A) The students will argue with her about her choice of statements.
    - (B) The students will think of a case that does not fit what she says.
    - (C) The students will think the animal world is impossible to study.
    - (D) The students will think she does not know what she is doing.

11. Listen again to part of the lecture. Then answer the question.
    What does the professor imply when she says this:
    - (A) Elephants have been known to kill people.
    - (B) Elephants are afraid of snakes, lion, and tigers.
    - (C) Elephants are only dangerous if they smell a person.
    - (D) Elephants are afraid of people, so they attack.

12 What is the main topic of the lecture?
- Ⓐ How dehydration affects the human body
- Ⓑ Some remedies for heat-related illnesses
- Ⓒ The differences between heatstroke and exhaustion
- Ⓓ The causes and effects of heat-related illnesses

13 According to the professor, what is dehydration?
- Ⓐ An illness of the digestive system
- Ⓑ The excessive loss of bodily fluids
- Ⓒ A type of fever caught from medication
- Ⓓ The excessive absorption of salts

14 According to the professor, how can heat exhaustion affect a person?
Click on 2 answers.
- Ⓐ The person will have a steady, slow pulse.
- Ⓑ The person might become unconscious.
- Ⓒ The person will sweat a great deal.
- Ⓓ The person will develop diarrhea.

15. The following statements list the symptoms of heat exhaustion and heatstroke. Click in the correct box for each sentence.

	Heat Exhaustion	Heatstroke
1 The person might exhibit confusion.		
2 The person sweats too much.		
3 The person will have a weak pulse.		
4 The person cannot sweat.		

16. What does the professor imply about heat exhaustion?
- Ⓐ It does not happen to people very often.
- Ⓑ People cannot protect themselves from it.
- Ⓒ It occurs in weather with high humidity.
- Ⓓ It is less dangerous than heatstroke.

17. Listen again to part of the lecture. Then answer the question.
What does the professor imply when she says this: 🎧
- Ⓐ The body easily absorbs fluids.
- Ⓑ Drinking fluids does not always help.
- Ⓒ The body needs constant fluids.
- Ⓓ Fluids must eventually leave the system.

How to Master Skills for the TOEFL® iBT

Actual Test
LISTENING 2

06

TOEFL LISTENING

Listening Section Directions

This section measures your ability to understand conversations and lectures in English.

The Listening section is divided into separately timed parts. In each part, you will listen to 1 conversation and 1 or 2 lectures. You will hear each conversation or lecture only **one** time.

After each conversation and lecture, you will answer questions about it. The questions typically ask about the main idea and supporting details. Some questions ask about a speaker's purpose or attitude. Answer the questions based on what is stated or implied by the speakers.

You may take notes while you listen. You may use your notes to help you answer the questions. Your notes will not be scored.

If you need to change the volume while you listen, click on the **Volume** icon at the top of the screen.

In some questions, you will see this icon: 🎧 This means that you will hear, but not see, part of the question.

Some of the questions have special directions. These directions appear in a gray box on the screen.

Most questions are worth 1 point. If a question is worth more than 1 point, it will have special directions that indicate how many points you can receive.

A clock at the top of the screen will show you how much time is remaining. The clock will not count down while you are listening. The clock will count down only while you are answering the questions.

PART 1 Conversation

TOEFL
LISTENING

1 What are the speakers mainly discussing?
- Ⓐ Why the student got a B on her exam
- Ⓑ Reasons why the student does poorly
- Ⓒ The student forming a study group
- Ⓓ The student's class participation grade

2 Why did the professor ask to see the student?
- Ⓐ He wants to give her an extra assignment.
- Ⓑ He wants to discuss her test and quiz grades.
- Ⓒ He wants to talk about extra-credit work with her.
- Ⓓ He wants her to work in the writing lab.

3 According to the professor, what is affecting the student's work?
- Ⓐ She works too many hours at her job.
- Ⓑ She studies too much for the exams.
- Ⓒ She does not care about the class very much.
- Ⓓ She cannot write an effective essay.

4 According to the professor, what should the student do?
Click on 2 answers.
- Ⓐ Join a study group for the class
- Ⓑ Speak more in class discussions
- Ⓒ Practice essay writing on her own
- Ⓓ Create an outline of her notes

5 What will the student probably do next?
- Ⓐ Drop the class from her schedule
- Ⓑ Go to the writing lab for some coaching
- Ⓒ Visit the classroom to find a study group
- Ⓓ Head home and go over her mistakes

Zoology

6 What is the lecture mainly about?
- Ⓐ Differences between South and Central American rainfcrests
- Ⓑ Exotic birds in the rainforests of the Americas
- Ⓒ The typical eating habits of the toucan and the quetzal
- Ⓓ The habitat and characteristics of the toucan

7 Why does the professor discuss the toucan's bill?
- Ⓐ To contrast it with the beak of the quetzal
- Ⓑ To explain why it has such a large one
- Ⓒ To show that it is smaller than a beak
- Ⓓ To indicate that it is only used for feeding

8 According to the professor, what is true about the toucan's nesting habits?
- Ⓐ It builds a nest on a tree limb.
- Ⓑ It uses the nest of another bird.
- Ⓒ It lives in the cavity of a tree.
- Ⓓ It does not need a place to rest.

9 According to the professor, what is special about the quetzal?
- Ⓐ It has metallic green tail feathers.
- Ⓑ It cannot survive in captivity.
- Ⓒ It does not live in small groups.
- Ⓓ It lives in North and South America.

10 The following statements list the characteristics of the toucan and the quetzal. Click in the correct box for each sentence.

	Toucan	Quetzal
① It only lives in the rainforests of South America.		
② Its tail feathers can be three feet long.		
③ Its habitat is in high mountain elevations.		
④ It mainly moves by jumping from tree to tree.		

11 Listen again to part of the lecture. Then answer the question.
What does the professor imply when he says this: 🎧
- Ⓐ The toucan and its sources of food depend on each other.
- Ⓑ The toucan takes complete advantage of fruit from trees.
- Ⓒ The diet of the toucan is limited to fruit-bearing trees.
- Ⓓ The diet of the toucan suffers from competition from other birds.

PART 2 Conversation

1 What are the speakers mainly discussing?
- Ⓐ How to increase the student's GPA
- Ⓑ Different tuition payment plans
- Ⓒ Applying for a school scholarship
- Ⓓ Various methods of paying for college

2 Why does the student visit the man's office?
- Ⓐ To pay a scholarship application fee
- Ⓑ To hand in her completed scholarship application
- Ⓒ To discuss her GPA with a counselor
- Ⓓ To inquire about various scholarship options

3 According to the man, why is the Wells scholarship a good choice for the student?
- Ⓐ It takes into consideration the fact he is minority.
- Ⓑ It completely pays for tuition and all textbooks.
- Ⓒ It often accepts students with low grade point averages.
- Ⓓ It offers an excellent work study program.

4 According to the man, what is the most important part of the application?
- Ⓐ Involvement in nonacademic school activities
- Ⓑ A relatively high GPA in core subjects
- Ⓒ The personal essay portion of the application
- Ⓓ The interview with the scholarship committee

5 What will the student probably do next?
- Ⓐ She will go home and start studying for a test.
- Ⓑ She will contact her old school for transcripts.
- Ⓒ She will write a check for the application.
- Ⓓ She will try to increase her overall GPA.

Business

6 What is the main topic of the lecture?
   Ⓐ The negative impact of monopolies
   Ⓑ The differences between a monopoly and an oligopoly
   Ⓒ Profit methods of the airline industry
   Ⓓ Different types of monopolies today

7 According to the professor, what happened to AT&T?
   Ⓐ It created a worldwide monopoly.
   Ⓑ It made huge profits from its long-distance services.
   Ⓒ The government had to break it up.
   Ⓓ The public boycotted its phone services.

8 According to the professor, what is price discrimination?
   Ⓐ Companies charge richer customers more.
   Ⓑ Companies implement different pricing levels.
   Ⓒ Companies increase their costs over time.
   Ⓓ Companies vary their prices with the law of demand.

9 The following statements list the characteristics of monopolies and oligopolies. Click in the correct box for each sentence.

	Monopoly	Oligopoly
1 A group of companies sets prices together.		
2 Utility companies are often a regional type.		
3 The airline industry is a good example.		
4 One company dominates the market.		

10 What can be inferred about pricing by monopolies?
- Ⓐ More competition would lower prices.
- Ⓑ Higher prices eventually lead to better quality.
- Ⓒ They usually charge all consumers the same prices.
- Ⓓ They have little control over the prices they establish.

11 Listen again to part of the lecture. Then answer the question.
What does the professor imply when she says this: 🎧
- Ⓐ People will not have any power.
- Ⓑ People should conserve energy.
- Ⓒ The cost is too great.
- Ⓓ The company will go bankrupt.

Biology

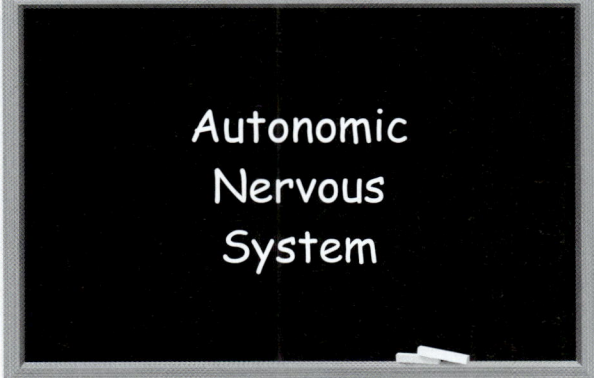

Autonomic Nervous System

12 What is the lecture mainly about?
- Ⓐ The limbic system and its main parts
- Ⓑ How defense mechanisms work in the brain
- Ⓒ The function of the sympathetic nervous system
- Ⓓ How the adrenal glands affect human emotions

13 According to the professor, what does the sympathetic nervous system do?
- Ⓐ It stimulates the brain to form memories.
- Ⓑ It relaxes a person during emotional situations.
- Ⓒ It prepares a person for a stressful situation.
- Ⓓ It gives a person extra time to deal with emergencies.

14 According to the professor, what is homeostasis?
- Ⓐ Body equilibrium controlled by the limbic system
- Ⓑ The process of releasing epinephrine into the body
- Ⓒ An active part of the brain controlling hunger
- Ⓓ An even balance maintained by the ANS

15 The following statements list characteristics of the sympathetic nervous system and the limbic system.

Click in the correct box for each sentence.

	Sympathetic Nervous System	Limbic System
1 The hypothalamus is a major part of it.		
2 It regulates adrenaline secretions in the body.		
3 It increases oxygen levels in muscle tissues.		
4 It plays a role in controlling hunger and fatigue.		

16 Listen again to part of the lecture. Then answer the question.
What can be inferred about the student when she says this:
- A She is tired.
- B She is scared.
- C She is depressed.
- D She is sick.

17 Listen again to part of the lecture. Then answer the question
What does the professor imply when he says this:
- A Difficult circumstances can let people do things they would not normally do.
- B People often find themselves in situations that are beyond their control.
- C She thinks that people can usually force their bodies to perform better than normal.
- D She has never seen a person do something amazing unless he was in a special situation.

Actual Test

How to Master Skills for the TOEFL® iBT

LISTENING 2

07

TOEFL LISTENING

Listening Section Directions

This section measures your ability to understand conversations and lectures in English.

The Listening section is divided into separately timed parts. In each part, you will listen to 1 conversation and 1 or 2 lectures. You will hear each conversation or lecture only **one** time.

After each conversation and lecture, you will answer questions about it. The questions typically ask about the main idea and supporting details. Some questions ask about a speaker's purpose or attitude. Answer the questions based on what is stated or implied by the speakers.

You may take notes while you listen. You may use your notes to help you answer the questions. Your notes will not be scored.

If you need to change the volume while you listen, click on the **Volume** icon at the top of the screen.

In some questions, you will see this icon: 🎧 This means that you will hear, but not see, part of the question.

Some of the questions have special directions. These directions appear in a gray box on the screen.

Most questions are worth 1 point. If a question is worth more than 1 point, it will have special directions that indicate how many points you can receive.

A clock at the top of the screen will show you how much time is remaining. The clock will not count down while you are listening. The clock will count down only while you are answering the questions.

PART 1 Conversation

1 What problem does the student have?
- Ⓐ She cannot afford to pay a school fee.
- Ⓑ Her room is unsuitable to stay in.
- Ⓒ She lost the key to her dormitory room.
- Ⓓ Her roommate is causing problems for her.

2 Why does the man tell the student about the intensive classes during winter break?
- Ⓐ To explain the likely cause of her problem
- Ⓑ To suggest that she sign up for one of them
- Ⓒ To point out how successful they are
- Ⓓ To argue that she should not blame the students in them

3 How does the man offer to solve the student's problem?
Click on 2 answers.
- Ⓐ By giving the student money to pay for the repairs
- Ⓑ By allowing the student to move her possessions next week
- Ⓒ By having the student stay at a nearby hotel
- Ⓓ By having a person come to fix the problem soon

4 What does the man ask the student to do?
- Ⓐ Complete some paperwork
- Ⓑ Show her driver's license
- Ⓒ Return an hour later
- Ⓓ Give him her roommate's name

5 What is the man's attitude toward the student?
- Ⓐ He is unconcerned about her problem.
- Ⓑ He is satisfied with her explanations.
- Ⓒ He is pleased that she is not upset.
- Ⓓ He is very understanding of her situation.

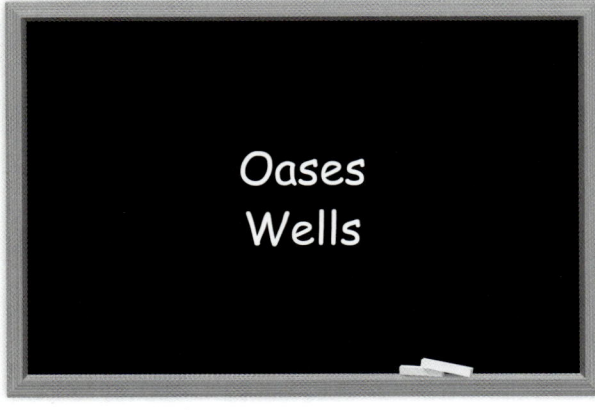

6 What is the main topic of the lecture?
- Ⓐ Why desert water is disappearing
- Ⓑ Sources of water in deserts
- Ⓒ Efforts to bring water to deserts
- Ⓓ Water in the Sahara and Arabian deserts

7 Why does the professor discuss the Amargosa River?
- Ⓐ To point out that it is an underground river
- Ⓑ To compare its path with that of the Colorado River
- Ⓒ To say that it has water for only half of the year
- Ⓓ To describe the unique ecosystem that it creates

8 According to the professor, how do people use oases in deserts?
Click on 2 answers.
- Ⓐ By irrigating crops with their water
- Ⓑ By bathing and cleaning with their water
- Ⓒ By stopping desertification with their water
- Ⓓ By using their water for animals

9 What does the professor imply about the Al-Ahsa Oasis?
- Ⓐ The water in it is sometimes salty.
- Ⓑ People cannot always drink its water.
- Ⓒ It has been shrinking in recent times.
- Ⓓ Agriculture is practiced around it.

10 Why does the professor explain what an aquifer is?
- Ⓐ To show how it is formed
- Ⓑ To explain how it can create oases
- Ⓒ To claim only the Sahara Desert has one
- Ⓓ To state how deep underground it can be

11 Based on the information in the lecture, indicate which type of desert water the statements refer to.

Click in the correct box for each sentence.

	Oases	Wells
1 Can be created with the use of modern technology		
2 May bubble up to the surface of the land		
3 May have water that is thousands of years old		
4 Are taken care of by people living in the desert		

PART 2 Conversation

TOEFL

LISTENING

1 What are the speakers mainly discussing?
- Ⓐ Reasons why solar and lunar eclipses happen
- Ⓑ A term that the professor discussed in class
- Ⓒ A paper that the student will write on syzygies
- Ⓓ The student's need to pay more attention in class

2 According to the professor, what is true about a syzygy?
Click on 2 answers.
- Ⓐ It can happen when three stars align.
- Ⓑ It can involve both planets and moons.
- Ⓒ It may cause an eclipse to occur.
- Ⓓ It happens rarely in the solar system.

3 What is the professor's attitude toward the student?
- Ⓐ He expresses pleasure that she understands a difficult concept.
- Ⓑ He feels disappointed that she does not listen well in class.
- Ⓒ He is pleased that she did so well on her recent examination.
- Ⓓ He is satisfied with her understanding of the entire course material.

4. What can be inferred about the professor?
   Ⓐ He will talk on the telephone soon.
   Ⓑ He will attend a faculty meeting next.
   Ⓒ He has office hours later in the day.
   Ⓓ He often gives quizzes to his students.

5. Listen again to part of the conversation. Then answer the question.
   What can be inferred about the student when she says this:
   Ⓐ She frequently visits the professor.
   Ⓑ She is embarrassed about her mistake.
   Ⓒ She does not usually ask questions.
   Ⓓ She is confused about a matter.

Architecture

6 What is the lecture mainly about?
- Ⓐ The historical background for Tudor Architecture
- Ⓑ A comparison of Tudor and Medieval Architecture
- Ⓒ Famous home influenced by Tudor Architecture
- Ⓓ The characteristics of Tudor Architecture

7 What is the professor's opinion of Tudor Architecture?
- Ⓐ It is the style that she likes the most.
- Ⓑ She finds it too ornate for her tastes.
- Ⓒ She loves the way that it uses wood.
- Ⓓ It does not have a big effect on her.

8 How is the lecture organized?
- Ⓐ The professor covers important events in chronological order.
- Ⓑ The professor takes questions from the students and then answers them.
- Ⓒ The professor shows pictures and discusses aspects of them.
- Ⓓ The professor describes some features by pointing them out on a model.

9 In the lecture, the professor describes a number of facts about Tudor homes. Indicate whether each of the following statements is a fact about Tudor homes.

Click in the correct box for each sentence.

	Fact	Not a Fact
1 They are usually made entirely with wood.		
2 They have steep roofs with many gables.		
3 They have entrances in their exact centers.		
4 They are constructed with wood frames.		

10 What will the professor probably do next?
  Ⓐ Show some pictures of homes in New York
  Ⓑ Discuss famous Tudor homes in England
  Ⓒ Describe the interiors of Tudor homes
  Ⓓ Talk about the construction of Tudor homes

11 Listen again to part of the lecture. Then answer the question.
What does the professor imply when she says this: 🎧
  Ⓐ The student should already know the answer.
  Ⓑ There is not enough time for her to respond.
  Ⓒ She will provide an answer to the question later.
  Ⓓ The student does not understand the information.

Astronomy

12 What aspect of the Kepler Space Telescope does the professor mainly discuss?
- Ⓐ The construction of it
- Ⓑ The ways that astronomers used it
- Ⓒ The various discoveries it made
- Ⓓ The reasons it could last for so long

13 According to the professor, what was the role of William Borucki?
- Ⓐ He encouraged NASA to make a space telescope to find exoplanets.
- Ⓑ He invented the technology used in the Kepler Space Telescope's cameras.
- Ⓒ He was the astronomer who discovered the most exoplanets.
- Ⓓ He acquired the funding needed to make the Kepler Space Telescope.

14 Why does the professor tell the students to look at their palms?
- Ⓐ To point out how many stars can be found in a small area of space
- Ⓑ To explain how the Kepler Space Telescope was able to operate
- Ⓒ To conduct an experiment on the brightness of various stars
- Ⓓ To show how much space the Kepler Space Telescope examined

15 Why does the professor discuss Kepler's Third Law?

Ⓐ To compare it with Kepler's First and Second laws
Ⓑ To explain how the telescope located exoplanets
Ⓒ To show the power of the telescope's cameras
Ⓓ To point out why astronomers look for exoplanets

16 In the lecture, the professor describes a number of facts about the Kepler Space Telescope. Indicate whether each of the following statements is a fact about the Kepler Space Telescope.

Click in the correct box for each sentence.

	Fact	Not a Fact
1 It found more than half a million exoplanets.		
2 It learned that most stars have at least one exoplanet around them.		
3 It found out that rocky planets are more common than gas giants.		
4 It was in operation for more than two decades.		

17 Listen again to part of the lecture. Then answer the question.
What does the professor mean when she says this: 🎧

Ⓐ It was only possible to operate Kepler for a year.
Ⓑ Kepler performed better than it was supposed to.
Ⓒ The price of building Kepler was too high.
Ⓓ Most people expected Kepler to be a failure.

How to Master Skills for the TOEFL® iBT

Actual Test
LISTENING 2

08

TOEFL LISTENING

Listening Section Directions

This section measures your ability to understand conversations and lectures in English.

The Listening section is divided into separately timed parts. In each part, you will listen to 1 conversation and 1 or 2 lectures. You will hear each conversation or lecture only **one** time.

After each conversation and lecture, you will answer questions about it. The questions typically ask about the main idea and supporting details. Some questions ask about a speaker's purpose or attitude. Answer the questions based on what is stated or implied by the speakers.

You may take notes while you listen. You may use your notes to help you answer the questions. Your notes will not be scored.

If you need to change the volume while you listen, click on the **Volume** icon at the top of the screen.

In some questions, you will see this icon: 🎧 This means that you will hear, but not see, part of the question.

Some of the questions have special directions. These directions appear in a gray box on the screen.

Most questions are worth 1 point. If a question is worth more than 1 point, it will have special directions that indicate how many points you can receive.

A clock at the top of the screen will show you how much time is remaining. The clock will not count down while you are listening. The clock will count down only while you are answering the questions.

PART 1 Conversation

TOEFL

LISTENING 00:10:00

08 - 01

1 Why did the professor ask to see the student?
- Ⓐ To discuss a poor grade she got on a test
- Ⓑ To say that the dean of students wants to see her
- Ⓒ To ask why she has not yet applied to graduate school
- Ⓓ To inquire about her plans for the future

2 What can be inferred about the professor?
- Ⓐ He is a professor in the Chemistry Department.
- Ⓑ He has known the student for three years.
- Ⓒ He is the student's academic advisor.
- Ⓓ He has class after speaking with the student.

3 Why does the professor tell the student about studying abroad?
- Ⓐ To explain what inspires some students to do that
- Ⓑ To advise the student to strongly consider doing it
- Ⓒ To point out how life changing it can be for students
- Ⓓ To indicate it will improve the student's language ability

4 What does the professor imply about the student?
- Ⓐ She asks good questions in class.
- Ⓑ She is majoring in Economics.
- Ⓒ She needs to study harder.
- Ⓓ She has the top grade in her class.

5 What is the professor's opinion of the student's father?
- Ⓐ He believes her father is an effective businessman.
- Ⓑ He thinks her father is a great inventor.
- Ⓒ He likes the way her father thinks.
- Ⓓ He considers her father a hard worker.

Environmental Science

6 What is the lecture mainly about?
- Ⓐ Volcanic eruptions and the damage they cause
- Ⓑ Some types of powerful natural disasters
- Ⓒ How humans can help ecosystems improve themselves
- Ⓓ Ecosystem recovery after volcanic eruptions

7 Why does the professor mention Vesuvius?
- Ⓐ To say the area around it has completely recovered
- Ⓑ To claim it was history's most destructive eruption
- Ⓒ To state that it is no longer active
- Ⓓ To point out how powerful it was

8 According to the professor, how can birds contribute to plants growing in regions affected by volcanoes?
- Ⓐ By building nests in the regions
- Ⓑ By dropping seeds on the land
- Ⓒ By migrating to and from the land
- Ⓓ By searching for food in the regions

9. According to the professor, what was the first organism to begin growing after the Kīlauea Iki eruption?
   Ⓐ Lichens
   Ⓑ Mosses
   Ⓒ Algae
   Ⓓ Ferns

10. What comparison does the professor make between Kīlauea Iki and Mt. St. Helens?
    Ⓐ The length of their eruptions
    Ⓑ The power of their eruptions
    Ⓒ The type of their eruptions
    Ⓓ The people killed by their eruptions

11. Listen again to part of the lecture. Then answer the question.
    What does the professor mean when he says this:
    Ⓐ The student should try to guess again.
    Ⓑ The student almost got the answer right.
    Ⓒ The student's answer is far from correct.
    Ⓓ The student is not paying close attention.

Zoology

Chimpanzees

12 What aspect of chimpanzees does the professor mainly discuss?
- Ⓐ Their eating and hunting habits
- Ⓑ Their socialization skills
- Ⓒ Their tendency to prefer meat to plants
- Ⓓ Their hunting methods using tools

13 What can be inferred about chimpanzee eating habits?
- Ⓐ They must eat a lot of food every day.
- Ⓑ They obtain all the nutrients they need from plants.
- Ⓒ They are capable of going without food for days.
- Ⓓ They do not consume very much meat.

14 What is the professor's opinion of chimpanzees?
- Ⓐ They are intelligent and can solve problems well.
- Ⓑ They are too violent and fight amongst themselves.
- Ⓒ They are the smartest of all primates in Africa.
- Ⓓ They are able to adapt to problems which occur.

15 Why does the professor discuss the red colobus monkey?
- Ⓐ To describe its eating habits
- Ⓑ To say that chimpanzees like hunting it
- Ⓒ To mention where it most commonly lives
- Ⓓ To compare its size with that of the chimpanzee

16 What can be inferred about chimpanzee hunting packs?
- Ⓐ They may go on hunts far from their territory.
- Ⓑ Large ones form to hunt other chimpanzees.
- Ⓒ The number of members tends to vary.
- Ⓓ They are active all throughout the year.

17 In the lecture, the professor describes a number of facts about chimpanzee hunting methods. Indicate whether each of the following statements is a fact about chimpanzee hunting methods.

Click in the correct box for each sentence.

	Fact	Not a Fact
1 It involves chimpanzees having different roles.		
2 There are usually some chimpanzees with weapons.		
3 The kill is normally made by the largest male.		
4 Only chimpanzees that hunt get to consume the meat.		

PART 2 Conversation

TOEFL
LISTENING

08 - 04

1 What are the speakers mainly discussing?
  Ⓐ The student's performance on her midterm exam
  Ⓑ The most recent lecture the professor gave
  Ⓒ An extra-credit report that the student submitted
  Ⓓ A topic for a paper that the student will write

2 According to the professor, what caused the poor relations between Spain and Britain before the Spanish Armada?
Click on 2 answers.
  Ⓐ Fighting between the two in their New World colonies
  Ⓑ Difficult economic times happening in some parts of Europe
  Ⓒ British privateer attacks on Spanish treasure ships
  Ⓓ Differences in religious beliefs between the two countries

3 Why does the professor mention Sir Francis Drake?
  Ⓐ To detail his role in the Spanish Armada
  Ⓑ To say that he successfully attacked Spanish ships
  Ⓒ To explain why he disliked the Spanish so much
  Ⓓ To point out his relationship with King Philip II

4 Listen again to part of the conversation. Then answer the question.
What is the purpose of the professor's response to the student:

- Ⓐ To request that she provide a source for her claim
- Ⓑ To state that she needs to do much better research
- Ⓒ To claim that she has come up with a new idea
- Ⓓ To indicate that she has some incorrect information

5 Listen again to part of the conversation. Then answer the question.
What does the professor mean when he says this:

- Ⓐ He does not like the student's topic.
- Ⓑ He agrees with the student's decision.
- Ⓒ He will not require the student to do more work.
- Ⓓ He would like to conclude the meeting.

Astronomy

6 What aspect of the Galilean moons does the professor mainly discuss?
- Ⓐ Their primary characteristics
- Ⓑ Their orbits around Jupiter
- Ⓒ Their liquid oceans
- Ⓓ Their chances of having life

7 What does the professor imply about Jupiter and Saturn?
- Ⓐ They are the two planets with the strongest gravity.
- Ⓑ They are larger than the other planets in the solar system.
- Ⓒ Astronomers believe their moons may have alien life.
- Ⓓ The number of moons they have will likely increase later.

8 How does the professor organize the information about the Galilean moons that he presents to the class?
- Ⓐ By talking about them based on their closeness to Jupiter
- Ⓑ By covering them according to the sizes of their oceans
- Ⓒ By discussing them from the largest to the smallest
- Ⓓ By focusing on the possibility that they may have lifeforms

9 Indicate which of the Galilean moons the following statements describe.
Click on the correct box for each statement.

	Ganymede	Io	Europa
1 Has hundreds of active volcanoes			
2 Has two space probes approaching that will explore it closely			
3 Has its own magnetic field			
4 Has a layer of outer ice around 150 kilometers thick			

10 According to the professor, why is the surface of Europa so smooth?
Ⓐ Because of the strength of Jupiter's gravity
Ⓑ Because of the liquid water beneath its surface
Ⓒ Because of the lack of impacts by asteroids
Ⓓ Because of the constant flow of lava on its surface

11 What will the professor probably do next?
Ⓐ Give the students a homework assignment
Ⓑ Discuss the upcoming midterm exam
Ⓒ Let the class take a break
Ⓓ Talk about one of Saturn's moons

How to Master Skills for the TOEFL® iBT

Second Edition

Actual Test

Answers
Scripts
Explanations

LISTENING 2

DARAKWON

Actual Test
LISTENING 2

Answers
Scripts
Explanations

ACTUAL TEST 01

p.009

Answers

PART 1

| 1 | D | 2 | C | 3 | B | 4 | D |
| 5 | C | 6 | D | 7 | C | 8 | B |

9 Formation: 4 Strength: 3 Safety: 1, 2
10 D   11 B

PART 2

| 1 | B | 2 | C | 3 | A | 4 | C |
| 5 | B | 6 | B | 7 | A | 8 | C |

9 Roots: 2 Bark: 4 Leaves: 1, 3
10 D   11 B   12 A   13 A
14 D   15 Western Europe: 2, 3
        Eastern and Southern Europe: 1, 4
16 C   17 D

Scripts & Explanations

PART 1 Conversation 🎧 01-01   p.011

W Professor: Good morning. Is there something that I can help you with?

M Student: Hello, Professor Jackson. I'm a student in your French 2 class that meets on Monday, Wednesday, and Friday at three in the afternoon.

W: Um, are you sure that you're in my class? It's very small. There are only about eighteen students in class, and I don't seem to have ever seen you before. Surely you must be mistaken.

M: ⁴Oh, no, ma'am. I am definitely enrolled in your class. My name is Richard Benson. You've probably seen my name on the class roster.

W: Richard Benson . . . Why does that name ring a bell? Wait a minute! You're the student who signed up but never shows up for class.

M: Um, yes, ma'am. That would be me.

W: Well, don't you think it's a little too late to be attending class now? After all, the semester is already five weeks old, and unless you were there on the very first day when I didn't take attendance, you have yet to appear at a single one of my classes. I'll have you know that unexcused absences weigh heavily upon your grade in my class. For every three classes you miss, you lose a letter grade. By my reckoning, I'd say that there's no way you can get anything higher than a D.

M: Um, actually, I have a pretty good excuse. I was, well, I was in the hospital for the first month of school. My doctor has just recently approved me to go back to class.

W: Oh, I see. Um, what exactly was the problem if I may be so bold as to ask?

M: I had a car accident that put me out of action for a while. But I'm much better now.

W: Well, that's good to hear. So it seems as though you have a legitimate excuse for missing so much class time. It would be improper for me to punish you for missing out when it was due to circumstances out of your control.

M: That's a relief. Thanks so much, Professor.

W: But . . . I must add that I'm rather concerned about your ability to, uh, you know, catch up with the rest of the students. As you know, classes in foreign languages build upon one another. It will be somewhat hard for you to play catch-up with the rest of the class. Are you up to the challenge?

M: Yes, ma'am. I think that I can handle it. I know that I'm going to work hard, but, well, when I was in the hospital, I had a lot of time to myself. It's pretty boring just sitting around, and I'm not really the kind of guy to spend all day online. So I hit the books while I was there. I know it's not the same as classroom instruction, but I feel like I did get a little learning done.

W: ⁵Well, you sound like just the kind of go-getter that I love having in my classes.

M: Thank you, ma'am. I won't let you down.

W: No, I don't think you will.

---

1 Gist-Content Question

Ⓓ The student and the professor mainly discuss the student's absence from class all semester.

2 Detail Question

Ⓒ The professor tells the student, "I'll have you know that unexcused absences weigh heavily upon your grade in my class. For every three classes you miss, you lose a letter grade."

3 Making Inference Question

Ⓑ The student says, "I know that I'm going to work hard, but, well, when I was in the hospital, I had a lot of time to myself. It's pretty boring just sitting around, and I'm not really the kind of guy to spend all day online. So I hit the books while I was there." It can therefore be inferred that he is motivated to do well in the class.

4 Understanding Function Question

  Ⓓ In stating, "Richard Benson . . . Why does that name ring a bell?" the professor implies that she has heard the student's name before.

5 Understanding Attitude Question

  Ⓒ In calling the student a "go-getter," the professor means that she believes the student will be successful in her class.

PART 1 Lecture 🎧 01-02   p.014

M Professor: **11 I guess it's no big surprise to those of you from this area that tornadoes are one of our biggest problems.** In fact, we have a special center for tornado studies here in our department. Today, I'll get you up to speed on tornado basics. Anyone interested in more advanced studies has to be at least a third-year student. Okay, uh, so what is a tornado, and how can we classify tornadoes? First, almost all tornadoes are associated with thunderstorms. I'm not talking about your little storm on a summer afternoon but whole lines of thunderstorms, the kinds that bring torrential rain and massive bolts of lightning. Tornadoes can also occur during tropical storms such as hurricanes, but most come from thunderstorms.

Tornadoes are spawned from a fast, rotating column of rising air inside the thunderstorm. When warm, moist air hits an east-moving cold front, a line of thunderstorms can form. Hot, humid air is pushed down by the cold, dry air on top, so it's like a layer of cold air over warm air. A change in wind direction and an increase in wind speed cause an, uh, spinning effect. This pushes a column of warm air into the air, causing a thunderstorm to develop. Inside a thunderstorm, the air can rise as fast as, uh, 150 miles per hour. We call this an updraft. This updraft rotates very fast, and from it, tornadoes spin off toward the ground. Now the conditions are not always right for tornadoes, and in different parts of the United States, they can occur at different times. For instance, in the South, they mostly happen in spring. But in the North, they mostly occur in summer. But don't be fooled into thinking any time or place is immune to tornadoes. They have been recorded in every state on the mainland and can happen at any time with the right conditions.

We measure tornadoes on what is called the Fujita scale. Let me spell that for you . . . F-U-J-I-T-A. Fujita. The weakest ones are classified as F0 on the scale. The big monsters are called F5, and if you ever see one, you'll remember it for the rest of your life. I saw one twenty years ago . . . It's still the most vivid memory of my life. It was more than a mile wide and destroyed everything in its path. It was estimated that its winds were at least 300 miles per hour. Now, not every tornado gets that big, and in fact, only about two percent can be called F5 tornadoes. Almost seventy percent of tornadoes are on the weak side, lasting fewer than ten minutes and causing very little damage or deaths. About thirty percent can be called strong and may last about twenty minutes, cause more damage and deaths, and have winds between 100 and 200 miles per hour. The most violent ones, the F4 and F5 tornadoes, account for almost seventy percent of all tornado deaths. Some have lasted for more than an hour and have traversed an entire state and well into another before dispersing.

Why they disperse so suddenly is still one of the things we're working on. Much of our work is related to understanding the mechanics of how they work and also in developing more early warning systems. It is true, without a doubt, from both my and many others' personal experiences, that more warning time saves more lives. People who have time to get to shelter usually survive tornadoes. Most deaths are caused by flying debris striking people. Some people have been sucked up and carried for miles, but this is rare. Underground is the safest place. If you can't get underground, get inside any structure, preferably one made of concrete or steel. Wooden structures get destroyed more easily and cause more flying objects in the form of wood splinters.

Now, there are a lot of, well, myths associated with tornadoes. One of the most common is that they don't go near water or mountains. That's nonsense. We've recorded them everywhere, in all kinds of terrain, and even in the desert and over water. Waterspouts are what we call tornadoes over the water. They can kill, too. Another myth is that you should open the windows of your house if a tornado approaches. This is supposed to equalize the pressure so that your house doesn't get destroyed. That's completely untrue. A tornado's winds are what destroy a house. It has nothing to do with differences in air pressure. You're better off spending your time getting to shelter than worrying about your windows. Always look for the warning signs. A dark, cloudy day with warm, humid air and a line of thunderstorms is a sure bet for tornadoes. Check your smartphone, weather apps, or the emergency alert system for warnings. We've got radar that can find them very easily when they form. Be prepared and be safe.

6 Gist-Content Question

  Ⓓ The professor mostly lectures on the formation and strength of tornadoes.

7 Detail Question

  Ⓒ The professor says, "Tornadoes are spawned from a

fast, rotating column of rising air inside the thunderstorm . . . A change in wind direction and an increase in wind speed cause an, uh, spinning effect. This pushes a column of warm air into the air, causing a thunderstorm to develop. Inside a thunderstorm, the air can rise as fast as, uh, 150 miles per hour. We call this an updraft. This updraft rotates very fast, and from it, tornadoes spin off toward the ground."

8 Understanding Attitude Question

B The professor clearly respects how powerful tornadoes are.

9 Connecting Content Question

Formation: 4 Strength: 3 Safety: 1, 2

The professor notes that tornadoes are formed by spinning updrafts in thunderstorms. As for their strength, tornadoes are rated on a scale from 0 to 5. Regarding tornado safety, the professor states, "It is true, without a doubt, from both my and many others' personal experiences, that more warning time saves more lives. People who have time to get to shelter usually survive tornadoes."

10 Making Inferences Question

D The professor says, "Anyone interested in more advanced studies has to be at least a third-year student." It can therefore be inferred that the students in his class are first- and second-year students.

11 Understanding Function Question

B In stating, "I guess it's no big surprise to those of you from this area that tornadoes are one of our biggest problems," the professor implies that the university gets many tornadoes.

PART 2 Conversation 🎧 01-03   p.017

M Employee: Hello. Welcome to the student housing office. What can I do for you today?

W Student: Um, I have a couple of questions about housing. You see, I'm going to be choosing a dorm for next year, and I'd like to find out about some of the, uh, amenities in each of the dorms if you don't mind.

M: Mind? Of course not. It's my job. We get lots of students in here asking about the differences between the various dorms. So fire away with your questions.

W: Wow. That's great to hear. Okay, well, I'm going to be a junior, so I guess that puts me in line for a decent dorm room, right?

M: You're right about that. Actually, juniors and seniors have the option of getting a single in a dorm as opposed to living in a double. Now, the price is a little higher. About . . . hmm, maybe six or seven hundred dollars a semester higher. Is that out of your price range, or should we keep discussing singles?

W: That's a good question. I'll have to talk to my parents about that. Why don't you tell me a little more so that I can be prepared when I speak with them?

M: Good thinking. It's always best to be prepared. All right, so let's forget about doubles and talk about singles for a second. Now, every dorm has singles. Of course, some have more than others. Personally, I think that Branson Hall has the best singles on campus. They're bigger than all the others, and Branson is a pretty new dorm . . . It's just a couple of years old, so it has the best, most modern facilities on campus.

W: Cool. I never realized that.

M: Unfortunately, seniors, since they get first choice, usually snap up all the singles there as quickly as possible. I'd say that you only have a, say, ten-percent chance of getting into one of those singles. It's a small chance, but a chance nonetheless.

W: Oh, that's too bad. Well, which dorms do most juniors typically stay in?

M: A very astute question. There are two of them. The first is West Hall, and the second is Henderson House. Oh, make that three. I forgot about Patterson House. Anyway, those three are always full of juniors.

W: What makes them so special?

M: [5] Location, location, location. They are all near the Quad, so they are within a five-minute walk of most of the key buildings on campus. Talk about some great places to be when you wake up ten minutes before your first class of the day begins.

W: Tell me about it. I could have used that today.

M: Oh, yeah? Well then you ought to consider seriously one of these places.

W: Great. Can you go into the details of each a little more?

M: Sure. Let me tell you about them. You know, you might want to write this down to make sure that you don't forget anything.

W: Yeah, that's a good point. Let me grab a pen and paper from my bag. Hold on a sec, please.

1 Gist-Purpose Question

B The student talks to the man about potential dormitory rooms she could live in.

2 Detail Question

C The man says, "Unfortunately, seniors, since they get first choice, usually snap up all the singles there as quickly as possible," about Branson Hall.

3 Understanding Attitude Question

Ⓐ The man is cheerful and eager to help the student during the conversation.

4 Making Inferences Question

Ⓒ When the man asks the student about paying for a dorm room, she responds, "I'll have to talk to my parents about that." She therefore implies that her parents pay for her schooling.

5 Understanding Function Question

Ⓑ The man mentions that the location of the dorms is important for when students wake up right before their classes begin. The student responds, "Tell me about it. I could have used that today." She therefore implies that she woke up later for her class.

PART 2 Lecture #1 🎧 01-04 p.020

W Professor: Hi, everyone. Our fascinating subject today is all about trees. Now, can anyone tell me what the two main types of trees are?

M Student: Ah, I'm not sure, but I think they are broadleaf trees and, like, Christmas trees, with needles and cones.

W: Close enough. Broadleaf trees are called deciduous, and trees with needles and cones are called coniferous. The deciduous is a form of what we call angiosperm, which just means that it is a flowering plant with seeds. Coniferous trees are gymnosperms, which is just another fancy word to say they don't have flowers but have cones. In fact, you could say that the cones are their flowers and seeds. Now, I will discuss the main differences between the two, and then I want to talk about the structure of trees in general.

First, let's look at the deciduous family of trees. They are our maples, elms, oaks, and so on, the ones in your front lawn and on your street. Their leaves are wider and broader than coniferous trees, change colors in fall in temperate climates, and drop off for the winter. Now they do this because they are really too fragile to survive winter. Coniferous trees, however, keep their needles all year long, oh, except for the oldest ones, which they shed. Examples of coniferous trees are pines, spruces, and firs. As I already mentioned, they have cones instead of flowers, and there are seeds in the cones, and these seeds can fall and turn into new conifers.

Okay, um, so those are the main differences. Deciduous trees have flowers, seeds, and broad leaves, which they drop in the fall, and coniferous trees have needles and cones and keep almost all their needles while sometimes dropping their cones. And they smell much better, don't they? Oh, I had a wonderful pine for Christmas this year. The smell is still fresh in my mind. Anyway, now on to the structure of trees.

Besides flowers, seeds, and cones, trees have three main parts that enable them to survive: their roots, their bark, and their leaves or needles. Roots go deep in the ground and absorb water up through the tree's system, which is very porous. Now, not all root systems are the same. There are two main types: shallow roots and deep roots. The shallower ones spread not far underground, are numerous, and are generally small in size. They sometimes even stick up through the surface of the ground. Some trees, like pines, have many roots but also a single main root, called a taproot, which goes very deep underground. This taproot can cause problems if someone tries to move the tree because, if you cut it, the tree will die.

The bark of a tree is in two layers, a thick outer layer and a thin inner layer. The outer layer is made up of dead plant cells, which the trees shed. The inner layer is living cells, but they too will eventually die. You know . . . there is a whole science dealing with the counting of bark tree rings. Specialists can determine if there was a great deal of rainfall in a given year by measuring the growth of the bark and the size of the ring. Of course, they have to cut down the tree to do this. Anyway, so the bark allows water and nutrients to be absorbed by the tree. It also protects the tree from losing too much water and from some diseases. However, in areas with lots of acid rain, the bark can be worn off, and the trees can easily die.

Leaves are the farmers of the tree and the givers of life to humans. If there were no plants on the Earth, we would all die from a lack of oxygen. Leaves perform two jobs for the tree: They produce sugar for the tree to absorb and remove water through evaporation. This is done by a process called photosynthesis. Carbon dioxide and water combine with sunlight and the green chlorophyll in leaves to make a chemical reaction that produces a sugar-like substance that the trees feed on. As this chemical reaction takes place, oxygen is a byproduct and is released into the air that we breathe. So trees do us two favors: They soak up harmful carbon dioxide, and they produce life-giving oxygen. I highly recommend everyone have a few plants in their home or dorm room. Not only will they make it look nicer, but they will also improve the quality of your air. **[11]** Unfortunately, man has not heeded the necessity of trees, and they are being cut down in record numbers. **While some logging companies replant them immediately, others are not so generous.** Of particular worry now is the Amazon Rainforest, one of our main sources of oxygen.

6 Gist-Content Question

  Ⓑ During her lecture, the professor mostly focuses on the purposes of roots, bark, and leaves.

7 Detail Question

  Ⓐ The professor says, "Deciduous trees have flowers, seeds, and broad leaves, which they drop in the fall, and coniferous trees have needles and cones and keep almost all their needles while sometimes dropping their cones."

8 Understanding Organization Question

  Ⓒ The professor talks about each part of a tree and discusses its purpose in her lecture.

9 Connecting Content Question

Roots: ②   Bark: ④   Leaves: ①, ③

About roots, the professor says, "Roots go deep in the ground and absorb water up through the tree's system, which is very porous." As for the bark, the professor notes, "You know . . . there is a whole science dealing with the counting of bark tree rings." As for leaves, the professor comments, "Carbon dioxide and water combine with sunlight and the green chlorophyll in leaves to make a chemical reaction that produces a sugar-like substance that the trees feed on. As this chemical reaction takes place, oxygen is a byproduct and is released into the air that we breathe. So trees do us two favors: They soak up harmful carbon dioxide, and they produce life-giving oxygen."

10 Making Inferences Question

  Ⓓ Based on the professor's comments, it can be inferred that the Amazon Rainforest is in danger from logging companies.

11 Understanding Attitude Question

  Ⓑ In stating, "While some logging companies replant them immediately, others are not so generous," the professor is pointing out that logging companies could do more to preserve forests.

PART 2 Lecture #2   🎧 01-05   p.023

W Professor: Now that we have discussed the origins of World War I, let's look at European society on the eve of war and, in particular, what were called the six Great Powers: Germany, Austria-Hungary, Italy, France, Russia, and Great Britain. These were the six nations that faced one another in the alliances before the war, um, with the Germans, the Austro-Hungarians, and the Italians on one side and the French, the Russians, and the British on the other. However, when war came, the Italians decided to, uh, stay out of it and eventually joined the Allied side with the British, the French, and the Russians.

But I'm getting, ah, how can I say, a little ahead of myself. I want to talk about society in Europe. It was a very class-conscious society, which means that everyone had a place and knew what it was, and most stayed in their place. In Britain, for example, one could easily distinguish between the working classes and the upper classes by their clothing, what they ate and drank, and their leisure activities. The upper classes drank wine, went to horse races, and played cricket, golf, and tennis while the lower classes drank beer and cheap gin and enjoyed boxing, football, and gambling. There was rarely any intermingling of social classes, with the upper classes serving as the leaders in politics, business, universities, and so on while the vast majority of the lower classes labored in factories and fields.

The Western European nations were more industrialized and richer than the Eastern and Southern states, which were more agrarian and had vast peasant populations, especially Russia, the most backward of the great powers. Italy, which suffered a series of drastic economic upheavals prior to the war, lost a great many people—perhaps as many as four million—to migration to other countries, most often the United States. Austria-Hungary was further divided by nationalities, with the German-speaking Austrians and Magyars of Hungary dominating the empire, leaving the Slavic peoples of Czechoslovakia, Bosnia, and the old state of Poland without much say in affairs. This was one of the leading causes of the war. Britain and Germany were undoubtedly the wealthiest and had much in common, with the kings of both nations being grandsons of Queen Victoria. The British relied on their navy, merchant fleet, and far-flung empire for wealth while the Germans, those industrious Germans, had a huge population, a massive army, and great wealth built on heavy industry.

Education was available to all children in most Western European nations, but going to university took money and, uh, connections. In Eastern and Southern Europe, universal education was not the norm, and many people—quite the majority actually—were illiterate. Uh, that is, they couldn't read or write. Almost all of our great literature of the war years comes from the university classes—almost always officers. The common soldiers wrote letters to their families, but there are very few cases of fighting men writing of their experiences after the war unless, of course, they were officers.

[16] Women, who would bear much of the burden of the war at home by taking the places of men at the front in factories and farms, were not even allowed to vote. **In recognition of the work women did in the war, in 1916, the British government passed a law that would allow women the vote but not until after the**

war was over. Imagine that! I guess they were afraid women would vote to end the war. It is without doubt that the war helped to speed the cause of woman's suffrage, and women were not to be denied the vote in most nations in the future.

Unfortunately, with all their education and class consciousness, the elites of Europe could not stop the war from coming. In fact, many of them and the common people rejoiced when war was declared. There were parades in the streets and marching bands, with beautiful girls kissing the soldiers goodbye and throwing flowers at their feet. Everyone thought it would be a quick war, and no one wanted to miss the excitement. Of course, no one knew it would take four years, ten million lives, and the destruction of the European order to end the war. **17** The upper-class officers led the lower-class men to a great slaughter. Their unwavering dedication to duty is very shocking to our society today. **Why did all those men charge the enemy in such futile battles? I think we could never have such a war again.** The people were innocent regarding war, not having experienced a major one for more than forty years before 1914. The unquestioning obedience to their leaders—even in the face of death—and their belief that they had to do their duty for their country.

12 Gist-Content Question

Ⓐ The professor talks mostly about the characteristics of European society prior to World War I.

13 Detail Question

Ⓐ The professor says, "It was a very class-conscious society, which means that everyone had a place and knew what it was, and most stayed in their place."

14 Understanding Organization Question

Ⓓ The professor closely examines several aspects of society in the lecture.

15 Connecting Content Question

Western Europe: ②, ③ Eastern and Southern Europe: ①, ④
About Western Europe, the professor says, "The Western European nations were more industrialized and richer than the Eastern or Southern states," and then adds, "Education was available to all children in most Western European nations." Regarding Eastern and Southern Europe, the professor notes, "The Eastern and Southern states, which were more agrarian and had vast peasant populations, especially Russia, the most backward of the great powers," and also states, "In Eastern and Southern Europe, universal education was not the norm, and many people—quite the majority actually—were illiterate."

16 Understanding Attitude Question

Ⓒ In stating, "In recognition of the work women did in the war, in 1918, the British government passed a law that would allow women the vote but not until after the war was over. Imagine that!" it can be inferred that the professor wanted women to have the right to vote immediately.

17 Understanding Function Question

Ⓓ In stating, "Why did all those men charge the enemy in such futile battles? I think we could never have such a war again," the professor implies that modern people do not have the dedication that people in the past had.

ACTUAL TEST 02

p.027

Answers

PART 1

1	Ⓓ	2	Ⓒ	3	Ⓑ	4	Ⓓ
5	Ⓑ	6	Ⓐ,Ⓒ	7	Ⓑ	8	Ⓒ
9	Ⓑ	10	Box Jellyfish: ①, ③ Portuguese Man o' War: ②, ④				
11	Ⓓ						

PART 2

1	Ⓑ	2	Ⓒ	3	Ⓓ	4	Ⓑ
5	Ⓒ	6	Ⓒ	7	Ⓐ		
8	Sensory: ③, ④ Motor: ①, ②					9	Ⓒ
10	Ⓐ	11	Ⓑ	12	Ⓑ	13	Ⓓ
14	Ⓑ	15	Ⓑ				
16	Crane: ③, ④ Ramp: ①, ②					17	Ⓑ

Scripts & Explanations

PART 1 Conversation 🎧 02-01   p.029

M Professor: Yes? Please come in.

W Student: Oh, hi, Professor Duncan.

M: Cindy Stephens. Welcome, welcome. What brings you here? Please have a seat.

W: Thank you. If you have a second, I want to ask you about my homework assignment.

M: Sure. I have all the time in the world. Did you bring it with you? You know, just to refresh my memory.

W: Of course . . . Here you go. I mean . . . I get your comments. I see how I missed the point of the assignment.

M: Let me see . . . Oh, yes. I remember now. The assignment was to compare two poems by Keats, correct?

W: Yes, Professor. We were to compare two, which I did. Still, I'd like to know why my grade is so low.

M: Okay, Cindy. Let's back up for a moment. Was the assignment simply to compare any two poems by Mr. Keats? Are you sure about that? Or was there a little more to it?

W: It was my understanding, as it was to a number of other students, that we were to . . . uh, let me check my notes, compare two poems by Keats by using specific examples from the text to support our arguments. That's exactly what you said in class. Oh, and the paper length was to be a thousand words maximum. I believe my paper was just over that number.

M: Really? Well, as I recall, Cindy, the assignment was for a comparison for two poems by Keats, but one was to be from his early work, that is, when he first began writing, and the other was to be a poem he wrote closer to the end of his life, uh, around the time of his tragic death. [4] I remember being very clear on that point for the assignment.

W: Are you sure? I don't mean to question you, but . . . I just can't remember you mentioning that in class.

M: Cindy, I'm sure I did. But even if I didn't, I believe it states so on your syllabus. You know, as I get older, I can't rely on my memory all the time, especially in class, where time is of the essence. This is why I always include specific directions for homework and papers and what not on the syllabus. Did you happen to refer to your syllabus for this assignment?

W: Actually, no, sir. I usually do, but this time I just went by my notes of what you said in class. Let me check really quickly. I have the class syllabus right here . . . Well, I stand corrected, Professor. Your syllabus states very clearly what you expect from our first homework assignment. How dumb of me! I feel so embarrassed. I'm so sorry for coming in here and basically accusing you . . .

M: No, Cindy, don't feel that way. It could happen to anyone. Look on the, well, the bright side. Your writing is excellent. You simply missed the point of the topic. [5] I'm sure that with next week's assignment you'll hit the mark. Just, um, be sure to, uh, check your syllabus.

W: **Well, thank you for your time, sir. And, yes, I will nail it next week.**

---

1 Gist-Content Question

Ⓓ The speakers mostly talk about the confusion of the student regarding an assignment topic.

2 Gist-Purpose Question

Ⓒ The student visits the professor to ask about the grade she received on her homework.

3 Detail Question

Ⓑ The student failed to refer to her syllabus regarding the assignment, which is why her grade was low.

4 Understanding Attitude Question

Ⓓ When the student says, "I don't mean to question you, but," she is trying not to offend the professor.

5 Understanding Function Question

Ⓑ The student says, "Well, thank you for your time, sir. And, yes, I will nail it next week." When she says that she will nail the assignment next week, it can be inferred that she is determined to do well on it.

PART 1 Lecture 🎧 02-02   p.032

W Professor: Remember that there are many different types of jellyfish, and, well, despite its name, it isn't exactly a fish. It actually belongs to the phylum cnidaria, as do corals, sea anemones, sea sponges, and the like. Jellyfish are a type of plankton, not fish, which means they are, for the most part, controlled by the currents of the ocean. They are about ninety-eight percent water. They have no brain and no bones and even lack a heart. The body of the jellyfish is gelatinous and therefore transparent, meaning that you can see through it. Its gelatinous body is one of its main defense mechanisms against its many predators because it makes the jellyfish transparent or nearly invisible in the water. That's a pretty good protection device. There's something else you need to know about the jellyfish in relation to its body: It is what we call polymorphic. If you break the word down, you'll get its meaning. Can anyone tell me what polymorphic means?

M Student: Well, *poly* means more than one, and *morphic* would be body or something like that, so polymorphic means more than one body . . . I think.

W: Good work. That's exactly what it means, and in the case of some types of jellyfish, it can exist as two different species in its lifetime: a polyp and a medusa. [11] The jellyfish starts out simply as a polyp, a cylindrical body with a mouth. This is the earliest form of its development. **Over time, it may develop into the latter stage, called the medusa, which is basically a network of tentacles extending down from the polyp body.** Now, the medusa is the second type of defense mechanism for the jellyfish, but this isn't all that it has. When it feels threatened or under attack from predators, it uses its tentacles as weapons. Lining the external wall of each tentacle are cnidoblasts. These are the poisonous stingers of the medusa. By the way, have any of you ever been stung by a jellyfish at the beach?

M: I was when I was young. I just remember that it really burned.

W: Well, that was the poison from the jellyfish's cnidoblasts. You were probably just unfortunate enough to get in its way or run into it. The reason is that they don't attack. Remember that they float around for the most part and have no real locomotion at all. They can use their tentacles for some propulsion, but they are used more for direction and guidance. Anyway, back to cnidoblasts. Besides stinging people at the beach now and then, they are really the jellyfish's second form of defense as well as a means of capturing food. The poisonous stingers contain a neurotoxin, which paralyzes prey, and then the tentacles are used to pull prey into its mouth.

M: But, Professor Keyes, aren't some jellyfish serious threats to humans? I mean, uh, I read about a guy getting stung and dying in Australia or somewhere recently.

W: Good point. And he's right, class. There are some that can be fatal. The most dangerous jellyfish to humans is the box jellyfish, also known as the Irukandji jellyfish. It's the type that stung the unfortunate fellow down under recently. Interestingly enough, it is only found in the waters off of Australia. It likes cooler water temperatures. And it is quite small—about the size of a coin—and has four main tentacles extending away from the main polyp. Its cnidoblasts are highly toxic and are even located on its main body. Once a person is stung, symptoms such as cramps, nausea, and high blood pressure can occur. Now, you might think that because of cramps, the victim might drown. This is unfounded. Let's remember though that most box jellyfish stings do not prove to be fatal, especially if medical attention is sought quickly. Actually, I believe most people who end up dying have some type of preexisting medical condition.

M: Wow, that's kind of scary, Professor Keyes. But what about the man o' war? Isn't that a kind of jellyfish, too?

W: It sure is. Actually, the Portuguese man o' war is a specialized colony of different types of polyps—four to be exact—which kind of latch on to one another. Each one is dependent on the other for survival. It really is a miraculous organism. It is highly developed for a jellyfish. Most commonly, the man o' war is found in warm waters, especially off the east coast of the U.S. The four types of polyps are for flotation, locomotion, digestion, and reproduction. The pneumatophore is the polyp that controls flotation and depth. Its color is usually blue or purple. Sometimes you can even see them floating up on the surface of the water with their many tentacles, called dactylozooids, floating underneath them.

6 Gist-Content Question

Ⓐ, Ⓒ The professor mostly discusses the makeup of the jellyfish and its defense mechanisms in the lecture.

7 Detail Question

Ⓑ The professor says, "The body of the jellyfish is gelatinous and therefore transparent, meaning that you can see through it. Its gelatinous body is one of its main defense mechanisms against its many predators because it makes the jellyfish transparent or nearly invisible in the water."

8 Detail Question

Ⓒ The professor comments, "Actually, I believe most people who end up dying have some type of preexisting medical condition."

9 Understanding Attitude Question

Ⓑ The professor remarks, "It really is a miraculous organism. It is highly developed for a jellyfish."

10 Connecting Content Question

Box Jellyfish: ①, ③ Portuguese Man o' War: ②, ④

About the box jellyfish, the professor states, "Interestingly enough, it is only found in the waters off of Australia. It likes cooler water temperatures. And it is quite small—about the size of a coin—and has four main tentacles extending away from the main polyp. Its cnidoblasts are highly toxic and are even located on their main bodies." As for the Portuguese man o' war, the professor notes, "Actually, the Portuguese man o' war is a specialized colony of different types of polyps—four to be exact—which kind of latch on to one another," and, "Most commonly, the man o' war is found in warm waters, especially off the east coast of the U.S."

11 Understanding Function Question

Ⓓ In stating, "That's exactly what it means, and in the case of some types of jellyfish, it can exist as two different species in its lifetime: a polyp and a medusa," and then adding, "Over time, it may develop into the latter stage, called the medusa, which is basically a network of tentacles extending down from the polyp body," the professor implies that all jellyfish do not develop a medusa.

PART 2 Conversation 02-03   p.035

M Student: Thanks for asking me here, but I just don't think I have what it takes, ma'am. I mean, sure, it has always been in the back of my mind, but I have never thought I am grad school material.

W Professor: Now, Jeremy, don't sell yourself so short. I think you would make an excellent graduate school student. You have been my student for how many years now?

M: Let me see . . . At least three years. Yes, I've taken one of your classes ever since my sophomore year.

W: And if I remember correctly, you've always been at the top of the class, have you not?

M: Sure, but, grad school? I mean, that is entirely different, isn't it? I would have to take the GRE, right? I did terribly on the SAT. I really don't want to have to go through that again.

W: Well, Jeremy, let me ask you this. What are your plans for after graduation?

M: I was just going to keep working at the bookstore. My supervisor said she would make me a full-time manager once I finished school.

W: But, Jeremy, is that what you want to do forever? I mean, I don't want to put your job down or anything, but the bookstore could hire anyone with a high school education for that.

M: Oh, I realize that, ma'am. No, I wasn't planning on working at the bookstore forever. I actually do have a plan . . . well, kind of. I want to save money for another year and then travel for a while. I've always wanted to travel, but I've never had the time or the money.

W: Yes, and I do think that is an excellent idea, but what about after the world tour? Back to the bookstore? What about a real profession, Jeremy? Something you would love to do for the rest of your life. You need a career.

M: [5] Well, to be honest, I've always wanted to work for a publishing company. As you know, I love to read and write. **To do that for a living, as in editing manuscripts and such, would definitely be my dream come true.** I don't need graduate school for that, do I?

W: Not at all. But the field is highly competitive. In publishing, an advanced degree would definitely help you secure a good junior editor position. Usually, applicants with just undergraduate degrees do lots of paper pushing if they are lucky enough to land a job at a publishing house.

M: I didn't think of that, ma'am. Do you mean that a master's degree could really help me out?

W: Sure, it could. And it would only take you a year and a half or so to finish a program. Personally, Jeremy, I believe you could even qualify for a scholarship. It would really be in your best interest to give it some thought. That's all I'm saying. Please understand that I'm not trying to force you into doing something you don't want to do. I just didn't know if you realized it is a viable option for you.

M: Well, I appreciate your concern, and I'm definitely going to give it some serious thought. I didn't know you had so much faith in me.

1 Gist-Content Question
  Ⓑ The speakers are mostly talking about the student's options after graduating.

2 Gist-Purpose Question
  Ⓒ The professor encourages the student to consider getting an advanced degree.

3 Detail Question
  Ⓓ The student tells the professor, "I actually do have a plan . . . well, kind of. I want to save money for another year and then travel for a while. I've always wanted to travel, but I've never had the time or the money."

4 Making Inferences Question
  Ⓑ The student does not believe he is good enough to go to graduate school, so it can be inferred that he lacks confidence in himself and his potential.

5 Understanding Function Question
  Ⓒ In stating, "To do that for a living, as in editing manuscripts and such, would definitely be my dream come true," the student implies that he has always wanted an editing position.

PART 2 Lecture #1 02-04   p.038

M Professor: One of the most ruthless viruses known to man—actually, one of the oldest ones as well—is the rabies virus. Left untreated, this virus takes no prisoners. Luckily, it has been all but phased out of countries such as the United States and in many places in Europe. Still, every once in a while, it rears its ugly head again. Worldwide, it is still a fairly major killer, considering that globally about seventy thousand people die from rabies each year. Of course, modern vaccines protect us from rabies and can even be administered after a bite by a rabid animal to counteract the virus. Yes, question?

W Student: Professor, you mentioned rabid animals. Do you mean that rabies can only be transmitted through a bite by an animal, or can humans get it in some other way, too?

M: As far as we know, the only way humans can contract the virus is by being bitten by an animal with rabies. The reason for this is that the virus is located in the saliva of the animal, which is how it is transferred from one animal to another. A bite is therefore the only way transference of the virus can occur. Good question.

Now, moving on, one of the reasons why rabies is so dangerous is that it is very, very sneaky. It is a stealth-like virus in that it is not easily discovered by the body's immune system until it's too late. Once an animal is bitten, the virus remains in the connective tissue of the skin and muscle, where it grows and multiplies in preparation for a future onslaught on the body's nervous system. Any virus that the immune system cannot pick up on its radar is potentially a deadly one. You see, the immune system monitors the bloodstream for threats and diseases that can harm us, but the rabies virus completely ignores the bloodstream in favor of the nervous system. [11] What's worse is that the incubation period for the rabies virus might be a month, but it could be as long as two or three years! **Imagine carrying that around with you for that long without even a whisper of a symptom.** Question?

W: Um, what do you mean by incubation period?

M: That was on our quiz last week, wasn't it, Lucy? Anyway, uh, I'll go over it again quickly. An incubation period is the time between the initial onset of the virus and when symptoms actually appear. Do you remember now?

Now, uh, where was I? Oh, yes, as I said before, rabies attacks the brain and the nerves, but let's follow its journey. Typically, a person is bitten by a rabid animal—most commonly these days, a dog—but it could really be any animal you come across, such as a raccoon or a bat. Bats are especially bad because many times their bites are not even detected. They have tiny razor-like teeth, which can cause minute, nearly invisible cuts in the skin but which are plenty big enough to give the rabies virus a wide-open invitation into the human body. Anyway, after the incubation period, the virus begins a slow journey to the brain. Once it is strong enough, it will enter a peripheral nerve, of which there are two kinds: sensory and motor nerves. Through one of these types, the rabies virus is carried to the corresponding portion of the brain. The result of this is very bad things.

This is when symptoms of rabies finally become apparent. If the virus attacks the sensory regions of the brain, symptoms such as numbness in the limbs or itching and burning sensations throughout the body will occur. Now, if the virus attacks the motor functions of the brain, perhaps you can guess what symptoms will arise, can't you? Yes, difficulty moving, paralysis, and even seizures are the most common symptoms. Now, at this point, rabies has infected the brain, and it will continue to spread rapidly through all of the other nerves. At this point, the animal will act in a very agitated or irritated manner—almost outside itself—like the stories you've probably heard about wild dogs or some other animals acting very erratically and strange. Well, this is rabies at work in its later stages.

After attacking the brain and weakening the rest of the body's nervous systems, it infiltrates the rest of the body as it is essentially looking for a way out in the same manner that it originally got in. Yes, saliva. Remember that viruses use the body as long as they can to survive and then attempt to move on. This is their ultimate aim: survival. In the final stages, rabies attacks the autonomic nervous system, or ANS, which controls breathing and blood flow and which will surely prove fatal for the animal.

6   Gist-Content Question

Ⓒ The professor mostly talks about why rabies is so deadly to animals.

7   Detail Question

Ⓐ The professor states, "Now, moving on, one of the reasons why rabies is so dangerous is that it is very, very sneaky. It is a stealth-like virus in that it is not easily discovered by the body's immune system until it's too late."

8   Connecting Content Question

Sensory: ③, ④   Motor: ①, ②

As for sensory functions, the professor says, "If the virus attacks the sensory regions of the brain, symptoms such as numbness in the limbs or itching and burning sensations throughout the body will occur." Regarding motor functions, the professor notes, "Now, if the virus attacks the motor functions of the brain, perhaps you can guess what symptoms will arise, can't you? Yes, difficulty moving, paralysis, and even seizures are the most common symptoms."

9   Detail Question

Ⓒ The professor remarks, "After attacking the brain and weakening the rest of the body's nervous systems, it infiltrates the rest of the body as it is essentially looking for a way out in the same manner that it originally got in. Yes, saliva. Remember that viruses use the body as long as they can to survive and then attempt to move on. This is their ultimate aim: survival."

10   Understanding Organization Question

Ⓐ The professor focuses on how the rabies virus progresses in stages.

11 Understanding Function Question

Ⓑ In stating, "Imagine carrying that around with you for that long without even a whisper of a symptom," the professor implies that a person may not be aware of having rabies for a long time.

PART 2 Lecture #2 🎧 02-05   p.041

W Professor: I honestly doubt that aliens came down in spaceships to help the Egyptians build the Great Pyramids or to do the job for them. There simply isn't any evidence to verify such a far-flung theory. There is some historical evidence to suggest how the pyramids were constructed, but even these, like the, um . . . I can hardly force myself to utter the words, alien theory . . . have yet to be proven or verified. So today, I'd like to go over a couple of the more popular theories in the scientific world on how these extraordinary structures may have been constructed. Yes, in the back?

M Student: So you are not completely dismissing the alien theory as a possibility?

W: [17] I really don't want to go there. As a scientist, I base my beliefs on proof and evidence, of which that theory has none. If you want to explore its possibility further, **I suggest you do your own research, but, personally, I believe it would be a waste of your time.**

　Now, let's get back to the pyramids. Remember that each was built with over two million stone blocks on average, and each block weighed at least two tons. This is a fact. This is measurable science, and it is undisputed. What this tells us is the task itself was enormous and required superhuman strength as well as ingenuity to achieve. One of the earliest theories was proposed by the Greek historian Herodotus, who claimed that armies of wooden crane-type apparatuses were used to lift and place the blocks in their given places. Now, while this is a fairly practical theory because we know that the Egyptians had created cranes capable of this type of work, there is a major problem with this theory. Does anyone know what that problem is?

M: Well, they would certainly need a lot of cranes.

W: You're on the right track. They would have needed thousands of them. There's no doubt about that. But think back. The cranes were made of wood. Most of Egypt then lacked great quantities of trees from which they could have extracted the material necessary to construct the cranes. In this case, they would have had to import the bulk of the material from neighboring countries, which would have proven very costly. Okay. So problem one is the lack of or difficulty in obtaining great quantities of timber.

　There's another problem as well. Remember that the pyramids averaged about five hundred feet in height. On the upper levels, there is not nearly enough space for the cranes to have been placed and anchored in to have been productive. As a result, for the most part, the crane theory has been put to rest for these reasons. It just doesn't seem practical. Now, the second theory on how the pyramids were constructed is the external ramp theory.

M: Professor Duncan, do you mean that the Egyptians built ramps to get the blocks up on the pyramid?

W: Well, that's what many scientists theorize. But . . . I'm not so sure that's the method the Egyptians actually used, and I'll tell you why in a second. First, some believe that long ramps were extended to each specific level of the pyramid, and scores of men pulled or dragged the massive blocks up onto them. Perhaps on the lower levels, this was possible, but it would have been impossible on the upper ones, where the steepness of the ramps would have been too great of an obstacle. Therefore, basic science tells us that the ramps would have had to have been extremely long to reduce the extreme angles for the upper levels and to have allowed the men to pull the blocks up. To say the least, these ramps would have had to have been over a mile in length. There is not nearly enough room or space in the area to construct them, nor is there any evidence that something like that ever existed.

M: But couldn't they have used ramps in a different way? I mean, they obviously had the manpower.

W: Yes, they did, and that's a good point. Some experts believe that they used ramps in a kind of switchback style that encompassed the pyramid construction site. This perhaps makes more sense than having one long ramp extending at least a mile away from the pyramid, but it has negative points as well. In order for the pyramid to culminate in a perfect point at the top, the corners would have to have been perfect, which would have called for very accurate measurements, which the Egyptians were obviously capable of. But with switchback ramps, the corners would have to have been completed last, and that would have made it impossible to measure accurately while the bulk of the pyramid lay under the network of ramps.

M: So how exactly were the pyramids created then if these two theories don't hold water?

12 Gist-Content Question

Ⓑ The professor mostly discusses three theories on how the Great Pyramids were built.

13 Detail Question

D The professor comments, "Most of Egypt then lacked great quantities of trees from which they could have extracted the material necessary to construct the cranes. In this case, they would have had to import the bulk of the material from neighboring countries, which would have proven very costly."

14 Making Inferences Question

B In stating, "Therefore, basic science tells us that the ramps would have had to have been extremely long to reduce the extreme angles for the upper levels and to have allowed the men to pull the blocks up. To say the least, these ramps would have had to have been over a mile in length. There is not nearly enough room or space in the area to construct them, nor is there any evidence that something like that ever existed," the professor implies that the ramp theory is almost certainly incorrect.

15 Detail Question

B The professor states, "But with switchback ramps, the corners would have to have been completed last, and that would have made it impossible to measure accurately while the bulk of the pyramid lay under the network of ramps."

16 Connecting Content Question

Crane: ③, ④ Ramp: ①, ②

Regarding the crane theory, the professor states, "One of the earliest theories was proposed by the Greek historian Herodotus, who claimed that armies of wooden crane-type apparatuses were used to lift and place the blocks in their given places. Now, while this is a fairly practical theory because we know that the Egyptians had created cranes capable of this type of work." As for the ramp theory, the professor notes, "First, some believe that long ramps were extended to each specific level of the pyramid, and scores of men pulled or dragged the massive blocks up onto them. Perhaps on the lower levels, this was possible, but it would have been impossible on the upper ones, where the steepness of the ramps would have been too great of an obstacle. Therefore, basic science tells us that the ramps would have had to have been extremely long to reduce the extreme angles for the upper levels and to have allowed the men to pull the blocks up."

17 Understanding Attitude Question

B When the professor says, "I suggest you do your own research, but, personally, I believe it would be a waste of your time," it can be inferred that she wishes the student did not care about a certain theory.

ACTUAL TEST 03

p.045

Answers

PART 1

1 Ⓐ   2 Ⓒ   3 Ⓐ, Ⓓ   4 Ⓑ
5 Ⓑ   6 Ⓐ   7 Ⓓ   8 Ⓒ
9 Ⓓ
10 Europeans: ②, ④ People of the New World: ①, ③
11 Ⓐ

PART 2

1 Ⓒ   2 Ⓒ   3 Ⓓ   4 Ⓐ
5 Ⓐ   6 Ⓒ, Ⓓ   7 Ⓓ   8 Ⓐ, Ⓒ
9 Ⓒ   10 Ⓒ   11 Ⓑ   12 Ⓑ
13 Ⓐ   14 Ⓐ   15 Ⓓ   16 Ⓓ
17 Ⓒ

Scripts & Explanations

PART 1 Conversation 🎧 03-01 p.047

M Student: Oh, Professor Anderson, I'm so glad you're in your office. I have something urgent about which I really need to speak with you. Do you have a couple of minutes to spare for me?

W Professor: What's going on, Eric? It sounds like you've got an emergency. I, uh, I guess I can be late for my faculty meeting. It's not too terribly important. Why don't you sit down and tell me what's happening?

M: Thanks so much, ma'am. So, uh, as you know, I've got to register for classes in a couple of hours.

W: Right. You and I worked on your schedule three days ago to make sure you get every class you want. Is there a problem we didn't notice?

M: No, there isn't. But, uh, do you remember I was planning to take the seminar in English literature with Professor Rawlings?

W: I sure do. You said you were eager to take that seminar on Renaissance English. And since English is one of your two majors, you must take that class to fulfill your major requirements.

M: Right. Well, uh, I spoke to Professor Rawlings today, and she told me she won't be here next semester because she just accepted a job at another university.

W: Oh . . . I wasn't aware of that.

M: Yeah, so I obviously can't take the seminar.

W: Do you know if the replacement professor the school hires will be able to teach the same seminar?

M: I asked, and she told me she had no idea. After all, she only gave the school notice of her upcoming resignation one day ago. She said there's no telling if the person who replaces her will teach that seminar, so she advised me to register for another one.

W: That sounds like good advice. Have you checked out the other seminars being offered in the English Department?

M: There are three. One is on modern poetry, another covers medieval literature, and the third is on American literature in the nineteenth century.

W: Which are you interested in?

M: None. That's the problem.

W: Well, you're going to be a senior next fall, so it looks like you have two choices. First, you can try to sign up for one of the other seminars being offered. Second, you can wait until the spring semester, which will be your last one, and take a seminar then. However, I should warn you that if you wait, there's no telling what seminars are going to be offered.

M: Yeah, I don't know what to do. Both solutions are less than ideal.

W: Hmm . . . Here's a third idea . . . How about going to the English Department right now and asking a couple of professors if they're planning on teaching a seminar next spring? After all, professors usually make plans a year or two in advance. If anyone says yes, inquire about the topic. If it's acceptable, wait until the spring semester.

M: That's a wonderful idea, Professor Anderson. I'm going to run over there now and do that.

W: What time are you registering for your classes?

M: At 4:30, so I've got two hours. Thanks a lot for your assistance.

W: You're welcome. I've got to run, too. Good luck.

1 Gist-Content Question

(A) The student visits to talk to the professor about a problem with his class schedule.

2 Making Inferences Question

(C) When the professor remarks, "You said you were eager to take that seminar on Renaissance English," it can be inferred that the student is interested in learning about the Renaissance.

3 Detail Question

(A), (D) First, the professor says, "First, you can try to sign up for one of the other seminars being offered." Then, she adds, "How about going to the English Department right now and asking a couple of professors if they're planning on teaching a seminar next spring? After all, professors usually make plans a year or two in advance. If anyone says yes, inquire about the topic. If it's acceptable, wait until the spring semester."

4 Understanding Attitude Question

(B) The student states, "Thanks a lot for your assistance."

5 Making Inferences Question

(B) The professor says, "I, uh, I guess I can be late for my faculty meeting," and then adds, "I've got to run, too," so she will probably attend a faculty meeting next.

PART 1 Lecture 03-02   p.050

M Professor: Spanish influence was really second to none during the early exploration of the Americas. The Portuguese were fast on their heels, but their goal was different from that of the Spanish. The Portuguese wanted to focus on building eastward trade routes to Southeast Asia for spices. They were not nearly as aggressive as the Spanish conquistadors. Portugal did end up gaining much of present-day Brazil while the Spanish occupied the remaining western areas of South America and Central America in the initial stages of exploration.

W Student: Um, I'm sorry for interrupting, but what exactly was a conquistador?

M: The root of the word is obviously "conquest," meaning to take over or to conquer. So we can gather that these early Spanish explorers were not benign navigators or explorers looking to make new friends across the ocean. On the contrary, they were often proven, decorated warriors given the task of finding fruitful lands and defeating any menacing or retaliatory groups defending or occupying them. Of course, one of the most notorious conquistadors was Hernan Cortez, who conquered the Aztec Empire in an act of aggression and slaughter, which ultimately secured the area now called Mexico for Spanish colonization. Now, of course, Spain's motivation was not necessarily land; it was simply a byproduct of its initial rampage, of which wealth was at its root. But this isn't all. Who can tell me where the Spanish first began their conquests?

W: Well, it wasn't actually the mainland of the U.S. I believe it was the islands of the Caribbean. Is that right?

M: [11] You are exactly correct. Most expeditions after Columbus began island hopping across the Caribbean, virtually exterminating the native peoples there either by sword or disease and doing the same once they reached the American continent. In the process, the Europeans introduced a number of new diseases, such as smallpox, bubonic plague, and influenza, to the native populations, which nearly annihilated them because **they had no natural immunity against these foreign diseases.**

Now, let's get away from the negative effects the Europeans had on the New World for a moment. We know that Spain was money hungry and that the Spanish discovered large deposits of silver in the New World and immediately sent much of it back to the homeland. But they contributed much to the New World, too, such as wheat, rice, sugar, coffee, pigs, and horses. On the other hand, the Americas contributed corn, potatoes, tomatoes, beans, tobacco, and even turkeys to the agriculture of Europe. In this way, each benefited greatly from the other because they were able to diversify their agriculture and livestock.

The Europeans were also not the only ones to introduce diseases to vulnerable people. Hepatitis was an early problem for the indigenous peoples of the Americas, and in time, it found its way onto ships and was slowly introduced to the populations of Europe. Of course, it was not nearly as devastating as the European diseases. Now, let's go back again to this silver influence. Picture it. Spain was mining and mining in the New World and sending shipload after shipload back to the European continent. Obviously, this large influx of silver had a major impact not only on the Spanish colony but on the European economy as a whole. Any ideas on its impact? Anyone?

W: Well . . . it probably helped fund further expeditions.

M: That's correct. These expeditions were not cheap by any means, and in many ways, they helped fund further ones if they were successful. Without the discovery and mining of precious metals, further exploration would have been hampered if not stalled for good. The influx of silver also promoted more long-distance trading in Asian silks and spices. As Europeans became wealthier, they became thirstier for exotic goods from the East, so they promoted and diversified European trade. Furthermore, the silver helped Europeans fund the agricultural development of sugar and coffee in the New World. Still, as silver began to pour into Europe, there was one negative effect that clearly outweighed all the positives . . . Mainly, a price revolution occurred, making the value of money decrease and the general prices of goods increase, causing major inflation throughout the major countries of Europe at the time.

W: But what about England, sir? How were the British able to enter the exploration or settlement race?

M: Excellent question. At this point, we are well into the sixteenth century, at Spain's peak of power and influence, but eventually, England was able to defeat the Spanish Armada, which opened the door for England. Population growth in Europe as well as a changing agricultural system also left England little choice but to look to new horizons. This, coupled with the surplus of unskilled labor, unemployment, and poverty and crime, soon led to England entering the race to the New World.

6 Gist-Content Question

Ⓐ The professor mostly talks about the effects of European exploration in the Americas.

7 Understanding Organization Question

Ⓓ The professor focuses on how the conquistadors were brutal in their behavior.

8 Detail Question

Ⓒ The professor says, "Now, of course, Spain's motivation was not necessarily land; it was simply a byproduct of its initial rampage, of which wealth was at its root."

9 Detail Question

Ⓓ The professor tells the class, "Still, as silver began to pour into Europe, there was one negative effect that clearly outweighed all the positives . . . Mainly, a price revolution occurred, making the value of money decrease and the general prices of goods increase, causing major inflation throughout the major countries of Europe at the time."

10 Connecting Content Question

Europeans: ②, ④   People of the New World: ①, ③

About the Europeans, the professor says, "But they contributed much to the New World, too, such as wheat, rice, sugar, coffee, pigs, and horses," and adds, "In the process, the Europeans introduced a number of new diseases, such as smallpox, bubonic plague, and influenza, to the native populations." As for the people of the New World, the professor states, "On the other hand, the Americas contributed corn, potatoes, tomatoes, beans, tobacco, and even turkeys to the agriculture of Europe," and also says, "Hepatitis was an early problem for the indigenous peoples of the Americas, and in time, it found its way onto ships and was slowly introduced to the populations of Europe."

11 Understanding Function Question

Ⓐ In stating, "They had no natural immunity against these foreign diseases," the professor implies that the natives often died from the diseases.

PART 2 Conversation 🎧 03-03 p.053

M Student: Hello. I'm trying to find a couple of books in the reference section, but I seem to be having some trouble locating them. You're the reference librarian, right? Do you think you could help me, please?

W Librarian: Sure. It would be my pleasure. Could you let me know what books you're looking for?

M: Oh, yes. I have the titles and the call numbers written down here on this paper. Here you are. Take a look, please.

W: Hmm . . . I know these two books. Doing a report for a psychology class, aren't you?

M: Oh, yeah, I am. You know, I'm normally pretty good at finding books in the library—I work at the engineering library here on campus—but the main library here is so big that it can get a little overwhelming sometimes.

W: Yeah, I hear that one a lot. Ever since we expanded last year, we pretty much doubled the available shelf space. We're still in the process of moving around books, so things do tend to get lost on occasion. Okay, uh, here we are. The books should be right here.

M: But they're not. I was just here myself. At least I wasn't looking for them in the wrong place.

W: No, no, you definitely weren't doing that. Okay, um, let me think about this for a second. Well, there is always the chance that someone put the books on the wrong shelf. We usually have people do shelf reading once a day, but it's entirely possible that the person made a mistake.

M: Why don't I look at the books on this shelf, and you take a look at the ones there? I mean, the person couldn't have messed up that badly and put the books too far away.

W: Right you are. Okay. Let's take a look and see what we can dig up.

M: ⁵ Hey, here's the first book on my list! I've got it. It was just one shelf over from where it was supposed to be.

W: **Well, it's a relief that you found the book.** But what about the other one? What was the title of it again?

M: It's called *A Student's Handbook of Basic Psychology*. Actually, that book is the one most crucial to my report. Without it, I'm sunk.

W: Don't worry. We're going to find that book. Since it's a reference book, no one can check it out, so it's got to be somewhere here in the library.

M: Are you positive about that? It doesn't seem like it would be too hard to sneak a book out of here.

W: Oh, no. Reference books have extra protection due to their high cost, and we've never lost a reference book yet.

M: That's good to hear.

W: You know . . . I've got a couple of ideas. One, someone could actually be using that book right now.

M: Yeah, I thought about that as well. What's the other idea?

W: Someone could have shelved the book in the circulating book section. Let's trot over there and see if my hunch is correct.

1 Gist-Purpose Question

C The student cannot find some books that he needs.

2 Detail Question

C The librarian says, "We're still in the process of moving around books, so things do tend to get lost on occasion."

3 Making Inferences Question

D The librarian states, "Sure. It would be my pleasure," when the student asks for help and also says, "Yeah, I hear that one a lot," when the student talks about the size of the library. It can therefore be inferred the librarian is used to people asking for helping finding books.

4 Making Inference Question

A The librarian says, "Someone could have shelved the book in the circulating book section. Let's trot over there and see if my hunch is correct," so the student will probably go to another section of the library next.

5 Understanding Function Question

A When the librarian says, "Well, it's a relief that you found the book," she is indicating that she is pleased the student found the book he wanted.

PART 2 Lecture #1 🎧 03-04 p.056

M Professor: The Sahara is the biggest desert in the world with almost all the other deserts able to fit inside its territory. The funny thing is that a lot of people think the Sahara and other deserts are, uh, completely sand and comprised of those long sand dunes that you see in travel documentaries or movies like *Lawrence of Arabia*. That's not so. In fact, there are many types of desert and desert formations, and that is going to be the topic for the rest of our class today.

Now, you may have the impression that all deserts are very hot, but we classify deserts into two types, hot and cold, and also base these classifications on their moisture content. I bet you didn't know that. Hot deserts like the Sahara have moisture or humidity levels of almost zero percent and a temperature range from just below zero degrees Celsius to almost sixty degrees. [11] Right here in California, we have one of the hottest deserts on the Earth with Death Valley having high temperatures around fifty-seven degrees Celsius, which means that moisture evaporates instantly. **It's a tough place, and whenever we do research out there, we bake like a bun in the oven. It's not for the weak of heart or mind.**

Cold deserts are those that are also extremely dry but have temperatures that can plunge to minus thirty degrees Celsius and don't go much above twenty-five degrees on the high side. The Gobi Desert in Mongolia is a perfect example of a cold desert. Colds deserts get much more precipitation, especially snow in winter months, but they are still relatively dry and cloud free compared to other temperate zones. The farther one goes into the interior of a continent away from the oceans, there is much less cloud cover and much lower humidity. For example, Europe has a humidity index of eighty to 100 percent, and Japan and Korea have long, hot, muggy spells in summertime. In contrast, the interiors of Russia and Canada are noted for their extreme dryness and bone-numbing cold.

In the desert, there are many types of formations that are created by wind and occasional flash floods. Sand dunes are the most familiar, with several different types. They are formed by wind blowing sand against an obstacle such as a cliff or a pile of rocks. Sometimes dunes form in the open and wander across the landscape, being blown in the direction of the, uh, prevailing winds. Now the most common dune is crescent shaped with a long, gentle slope on the wind side and a steep slope on the lee side, or the side away from the wind. These dunes can be up to forty meters high and as many as 400 meters long. Other dune types are formed by the wind moving in two different directions. This forms very long parallel dunes. Still others can be shaped like a pyramid.

There is a lot of sand in deserts compared to other areas, but in fact, most deserts have very little sand as a percentage of their total area. In the Sahara, only one-seventh of the total desert area is sand dunes. The rest is rock as the sand has been mostly blown away. If you just used humidity as a gauge of what a desert is, you could call the Arctic and Antarctic deserts although you'll never see a grain of sand there. So sand does not a desert make.

Wind and water also create many beautiful desert formations. Deserts record extreme temperatures between day and night. Any moisture in rocks is turned to frost at night and can break rocks easily. Great rivers such as the Colorado River here in the Southwest have also carved steep canyons, like the Grand Canyon, in desert areas. Mesas are another formation, uh, desert formation, that most Americans recognize from our own deserts. A high plateau of rock is worn down by centuries of wind and water, creating many formations. Deep water channels called wadis are formed, which isolates different parts of the plateau. They become buttes and larger mesas. Mesas have hard central rock that was once surrounded by softer rock that has been eroded and which falls around the base of the mesa to form a surrounding slope. The rock material that falls is called scree. Buttes are like mesas but smaller.

Mushroom-type rock formations are created by the wind blowing sand at ground level. This wears away the rock near the ground so that it is much thinner than the rock higher up, giving a mushroom-like appearance. Other bizarre formations like Elephant Rock in Nevada are the result of wind and sand acting to erode away the softer rock and have made some of nature's most beautiful sculptures.

6 Gist-Content Question

Ⓒ, Ⓓ The professor mainly talks about different types of deserts and various desert formations.

7 Gist-Purpose Question

Ⓓ The professor says, "In fact, most deserts have very little sand as a percentage of their total area. In the Sahara, only one seventh of the total desert area is sand dunes. The rest is rock as the sand has been mostly blown away. If you just used humidity as a gauge of what a desert is, you could call the Arctic and Antarctic deserts although you'll never see a grain of sand there. So sand does not a desert make."

8 Detail Question

Ⓐ, Ⓒ The professor notes, "Sand dunes are the most familiar, with several different types. They are formed by wind blowing sand against an obstacle such as a cliff or a pile of rocks," and also states, "Mushroom-type rock formations are created by the wind blowing sand at ground level. This wears away the rock near the ground so that it is much thinner than the rock higher up, giving a mushroom-like appearance. Other bizarre formations like Elephant Rock in Nevada are the result of wind and sand acting to erode away the softer rock."

9 Understanding Organization Question

Ⓒ The professor examines various characteristics of deserts in detail in the lecture.

10 Detail Question

Ⓒ The professor tells the class, "Mesas have hard central rock that was once surrounded by softer rock that has been eroded and which falls around the base of the mesa to form a surrounding slope."

11 Understanding Attitude Question

Ⓑ In stating, "It's a tough place, and whenever we do research out there, we bake like a bun in the oven. It's not for the weak of heart or mind," the professor means that people must be physically and mentally prepared for the heat in deserts.

PART 2 Lecture #2   03-05   p.059

W Professor: The snake is one of the most feared creatures on our planet. It may seem strange, considering that, compared to say, car accidents and murders, snakes attack and kill very few people in the United States each year. There are perhaps fewer than ten deaths in any given year. So why are we afraid of them? Perhaps it's the suddenness with which snakes can attack, by surprise, and their reptilian appearance. And outside of the United States, snakes do kill a large number of people. For example, they may kill 10,000 or more people in India each year. Tigers and lions also kill, but they are just big furry cats and in zoos. Anyway, so they, um, I mean snakes, are to be feared. My main focus today is on snakes in general, what kinds of snakes there are, and their major characteristics.

Most people distinguish between venomous and nonvenomous snakes, and that's a good place to begin. Excuse me. Let's start right here in our own country. There are perhaps over 2,000 species of snakes, and most are nonvenomous. Among the more common nonvenomous snakes is the garter snake. In the United States, there are four types of venomous snakes: rattlesnakes, copperheads, coral snakes, and cottonmouths. However, there are twenty-two species of venomous snakes, so, uh, all of them belong to the four types I just named. With the exception of Alaska and Hawaii, rattlesnakes can be found in every state. In fact, Hawaii has no native snakes at all. So if you have a real phobia about snakes, I suggest you move to Hawaii. There are many species of rattlesnakes, and they all have the unique feature of a rattle at the end of their tails. Its many hard cartilage pieces hit one another to produce the rattling sound. The rattlesnake is a member of the viper family of snakes, as are the copperhead and the cottonmouth, which are mostly found in the Southeast. The coral snake has two types, the eastern and western, and is distinguished by the very colorful bands around its body.

Around the world, the deadliest snake is the cobra in its many variations. It is responsible for more deaths in Africa and India than any other snake. Some cobras can even spit venom at their intended victims. In Australia, there are nine of the ten most venomous snakes in the world. It is estimated that the taipan snake has enough venom in one bite to kill over 200,000 mice. South America also has its share of venomous snakes but is perhaps more famous for having the largest snake in the world, the anaconda, which is not venomous. This snake is still dangerous though because it's a member of the constrictor family like the python of Southeast Asia. Constrictors wrap their bodies around their victims and squeeze them to death.

Now, a snake does not chew its prey. It has lots of teeth, and there are those dangerous fangs on the venomous ones, but a snake cannot chew its food. After it injects venom, squeezes, or bites its prey to death, it has the unique ability to unhinge its jaw and to swallow its prey whole. This process may take several minutes, but after that, the prey is inside the snake's belly. The belly will be distended, and the snake will not need to eat again for several days. Some snakes can eat dogs and pigs whole while the largest can even consume humans. A snake's digestive tract absorbs everything, including flesh, organs, and bones. Birds and mice are some of snakes' favorite prey animals. People are always wary when going to garbage dumps in Africa and India because cobras tend to hang around them to kill rats.

The snake is a cold-blooded animal, which means its body has no internal mechanism for adjusting its temperature, like humans and other mammals. The snake, like all reptiles, is influenced by the external temperature. I mean, when it's cold outside, the snake will be just as cold. This is a big reason why you don't see snakes in very cold places. ¹⁵ Heat doesn't seem to affect them as much as cold, but even in desert areas, snakes will be near shade most of the time and also near sources of water. Rocky areas are a favorite hiding place as well as inside dead trees. **Be careful when hiking anywhere and never stick your hand into a dark opening without shining a flashlight inside first to make sure it's empty.**

Another characteristic of snakes is that they shed their skins. As they grow, they get bigger, and their outer layer of skin peels away from their bodies. The snake accomplishes this by rubbing against an object like a rock or tree. Some anacondas have grown over fifty feet long, but most snakes are in the one-to-ten-foot range. Some of the smallest snakes are the most lethal, so don't let size fool you.

12 Gist-Content Question

Ⓑ The professor mostly discusses the physical characteristics of snakes.

13 Understanding Organization Question

Ⓐ The professor points out an interesting fact about snakes in stating, "With the exception of Alaska and Hawaii, rattlesnakes can be found in every state. In fact, Hawaii has no native snakes at all. So if you have a real phobia about snakes, I suggest you move to Hawaii."

14 Detail Question

Ⓐ The professor remarks, "After it injects venom, squeezes, or bites its prey to death, it has the unique ability to unhinge its jaw and to swallow its prey whole."

15 Understanding Organization Question

Ⓓ The professor mainly discusses American venomous snakes and where they are.

16 Understanding Attitude Question

Ⓓ The professor notes to the students at times that snakes are dangerous, so the students should be careful.

17 Understanding Function Question

Ⓒ In stating, "Be careful when hiking anywhere and never stick your hand into a dark opening without shining a flashlight inside first to make sure it's empty," the professor implies that a snake could be in a hole if it is dark.

ACTUAL TEST 04
p.063

Answers

PART 1

1 Ⓓ 2 Ⓑ 3 Ⓐ 4 Ⓑ
5 Ⓑ 6 Ⓑ 7 Ⓐ 8 Ⓐ
9 Ⓓ
10 Event 1: Ⓑ Event 2: Ⓐ Event 3: Ⓔ Event 4: Ⓒ
11 Ⓒ 12 Ⓒ 13 Ⓑ 14 Ⓑ
15 Ⓑ 16 Sarcasm: ①, ② Irony: ③, ④
17 Ⓑ

PART 2

1 Ⓐ 2 Ⓒ 3 Ⓒ 4 Ⓑ
5 Ⓓ 6 Ⓒ 7 Ⓓ 8 Ⓒ
9 Saccharin: ①, ④ Aspartame: ②, ③
10 Ⓐ 11 Ⓑ

Scripts & Explanations

PART 1 Conversation 🎧 04-01   p.065

W Student: ⁴Professor Dyson, you're having your office hours now, aren't you? I'd really love to talk with you for a couple of minutes if you could spare the time.

M Professor: Oh, hi, Mindy. You're always welcome in my office even if I'm not having office hours.

W: Oh, it's so nice of you to say that, Professor.

M: So what can I do for you today?

W: Well, you see, it's my paper. You know . . . the one that you assigned to us earlier in the week.

M: Getting an early start I see. I seem to remember that it's not due for another month. You sure are diligent, Mindy. I'll give you that.

W: Oh, thank you, sir. I just like to get started early on my projects in case I run into any trouble. That way, I can get all the problems out of the way and have an easy time finishing everything.

M: Yes, I was once like you myself. It's the best way to do things really. Anyway, what exactly do you need to know about the paper? The length? The approach? Or even the number of sources that you need to use?

W: Well, I have been trying to come up with a topic, and I think I have a couple of good ones, but I want to check with you first to make sure that I'm on the right track.

M: Okay. Then why don't you fill me in on your first topic?

W: Sure thing. Since we're investigating ancient pottery-making methods, I thought that I'd take a look at how the Romans developed their own pottery. You know, I was, uh, really impressed with last week's class on Roman artwork. I never knew they had such advanced pottery-making skills, so I kind of thought that I'd investigate it a little more.

M: All right. That's a very good approach. So your general topic is Roman pottery. Now, exactly what aspect of it are you going to discuss? Remember that since you're an upperclassman, I'm going to expect more from you on this paper than I would from a freshman.

W: I'll keep that in mind. But, uh, that's the problem right now. I was totally fascinated by that lecture, but I simply lack the knowledge base even to get started on coming up with a topic to write on.

Answers and Explanations **19**

M: Yes, I see your point. It's unfortunate, but most art historians focus on more modern times, so your education on ancient methods is probably a little lacking. Hmm, let me see what you could get started on. Well . . . there is always the Greek influence. You could take a closer look at that.

W: The Greek influence?

M: Oh, yes. The Greeks had a, well, a tremendous influence on Roman pottery making. Remember that the two were just across the sea from each other. ⁵There was a lot of cross-cultural interaction going on. Why don't you think about that aspect for your paper? **There's a fairly large corpus on this influence,** so you shouldn't have too many problems in finding what you need.

W: Excellent. I'll get on it right away. Thanks so much.

M: My pleasure.

1 Gist-Content Question
Ⓓ The speakers mostly talk about an upcoming assignment.

2 Detail Question
Ⓑ The student asks for help from the professor in finding a topic for her report.

3 Making Inferences Question
Ⓐ When the student says she will get started on her research right away, it means she will probably visit the library next.

4 Understanding Attitude Question
Ⓑ When the professor tells the student, "You're always welcome in my office even if I'm not having office hours," it can be inferred that he enjoys it when the student visits him.

5 Understanding Function Question
Ⓑ In stating, "There's a fairly large corpus on this influence," the professor implies that the library has many books on a certain topic.

PART 1 Lecture #1   🎧 04-02   p.068

M Professor: In our last class, we finished talking about the Mexican-American War, which ended with Mexico ceding the land that became Arizona, New Mexico, Nevada, and California to the United States. This was the second biggest expansion of the United Sates after the Louisiana Purchase in the early nineteenth century. Even before the war ended, the value of California was significantly raised by the discovery of gold there. Now, in those days, gold could be dug or found by individuals who staked out a piece of land or river and paid for the mineral rights. As long as a person worked the land, his claim was valid. This was a holdover from Mexico's mining customs since the land was Mexican up to that point. Nowadays, big companies have most of the possible gold fields already staked out. But the California Gold Rush, as it came to be called, produced a wave of migration to the west coast of the United Sates that hastened the entry of California as a member of the Union.

¹¹Gold was first found in January 1848, on the American River in the Sierra Nevada hills near Coloma. It was found in the river by some men who were building a lumber mill for a man named Sutter. So it has become known in history as the Sutter's Mill gold find. **Sutter and the other men tried to keep it a secret, but rumors spread, and by the spring of 1848, the word was out in San Francisco.** Men literally dropped their work tools and headed for the American River in the hope of striking it rich. The news reached the east coast by the summer, and President James Polk confirmed the rumors in December 1848. Then, the rush was on.

San Francisco became the base of, uh, I guess you could say the base of operations. The tiny settlement exploded from about 1,000 people to more than 25,000 within two years. Merchants moved in to make profits off the miners. The miners' nickname was the forty-niners since they went there in 1849. Now San Francisco has a football team with the same name. Anyway, men came to get rich, and some did, but most didn't. Many lost everything, including their lives in squabbles over miner's rights and stakes they had claimed. Just getting to California was extremely difficult since there was no intercontinental railway. Sailing around South America, a several-month's-long voyage, was fatal for many prospectors. Others sailed to Panama, crossed the danger-ridden isthmus to the Pacific side, and then sailed for San Francisco. There is no doubt that the building of the railway was given impetus by the discovery of gold in California.

Besides the railroad, the discovery of gold had other effects. An interesting side note is that blue jeans were first made during the gold rush. Levi Strauss realized the workers needed tough pants for working in the gold fields. He had a large shipment of a blue material from France called denim, so he made it into pants, and blue jeans were born. The most significant result for the United Sates was that California became a state. Thousands of people descended on the land from other parts of the country and even around the world. Now, as I mentioned earlier, the land had been part of Mexico and was still operating under Mexican customs. Sometimes there were disagreements over certain valued areas, and men weren't above murder to get what they wanted. It was a savage time, and even Native Americans were driven from their lands by gold-hungry prospectors. Technically, the gold was being taken from land that now officially belonged to the United States government. Soon, it became obvious that some control was needed, and law officers were hired and a government set up. Soon, there were enough residents to apply for statehood. On September 9, 1850, California became the thirty-first state in the Union.

Did anyone make a profit? Well, certainly, the first people to reach the fields and to make big discoveries did. Later, people had a harder time, and by the mid-1850s, almost all the easily accessible gold was taken. Only with a lot of capital and large groups of laborers could someone get to digging up the less accessible gold. Merchants perhaps profited the most from the gold rush by selling equipment to prospectors and by providing supplies and lodgings. The long-term results of the California Gold Rush are easy to see. The expansion of the American railway system to the west coast was the biggest. The inclusion of California as a state and the increase in immigration were also results. After the gold rush came a second rush of immigrants seeking land for farming, and I guess you can call this second rush an agricultural rush. But it all came, both agriculture and gold, at the expense of the Native American people, whose numbers were thinned by disease, starvation, and outright murder.

6 Gist-Content Question

(B) The professor mostly discusses the results of the discovery of gold in California.

7 Understanding Organization Question

(A) The professor states, "Now, in those days, gold could be dug or found by individuals who staked out a piece of land or river and paid for the mineral rights. As long as a person worked the land, his claim was valid. This was a holdover from Mexico's mining customs since the land was Mexican up to that point."

8 Detail Question

(A) The professor says, "But it all came, both agriculture and gold, at the expense of the Native American people, whose numbers were thinned by disease, starvation, and outright murder."

9 Understanding Organization Question

(D) The professor discusses various events and their results in the lecture.

10 Connecting Content Question

Event 1: (B) Event 2: (A) Event 3: (E) Event 4: (C)

First, the professor states, "Gold was first found in January 1848, on the American River in the Sierra Nevada hills near Coloma. It was found in the river by some men who were building a lumber mill for a man named Sutter. So it has become known in history as the Sutter's Mill gold find." Then, the professor notes, "The news reached the east coast by the summer, and President James Polk confirmed the rumors in December 1848. Then, the rush was on." After that, he says, "The miners' nickname was the forty-niners since they went there in 1849." Last, he remarks, "On September 9, 1850, California became the thirty-first state in the Union."

11 Understanding Function Question

(C) In stating, "Sutter and the other men tried to keep it a secret, but rumors spread, and by the spring of 1848, the word was out in San Francisco," the professor means that even though Sutter tried hard not to tell anyone, people still found out about the gold.

PART 1 Lecture #2 04-03   p.071

W Professor: Now that we've gone over the basic literary terms of symbolism, that is, metaphor and oxymoron, I'd like to go into a more detailed explanation of the literary technique of irony. You've all heard of irony before, right? Yes, I see that most of you are nodding your heads. That's good. Well, most authors like to employ irony now and then in their work to give it another layer or two of understanding, not just a surface or superficial one. It can make their work more substantial. But irony is not always so easy to detect. It takes real practice in recognizing some of the more subtle irony penned by crafty writers. Yes, question?

M Student: Yes, um, I think most of us have a decent understanding of what you mean by irony, but could you please give us a formal definition of it?

W: That's not a problem at all. I probably should have done that from the start, shouldn't I? Well, irony in literature is typically defined as a verbal play on words or a situational expression different from or even completely the opposite of what the reader is expecting. Key to irony is its unexpected presence. That is, um, we rarely see it coming. Good authors will blindside us with something completely surprising. Irony can come in the form of a single sentence or appear throughout an entire play, novel, or poem. It is not restricted to a few words. It can also be quite revealing of the author's own attitude or perspective, which is why irony is often so important in our understanding of a literary work. Yes? You have another question for me?

M: Okay, Professor Carter, I get irony, but isn't sarcasm the same thing?

W: Another excellent question I might add. Sarcasm is similar to irony in that it relates the unexpected and the obvious. But sarcasm is usually more direct, bitter, biting, and obvious to the reader or listener while irony can be much more ambiguous and veiled. I hope that clears it up for you.

Of course, irony is not always humorous. It can bite, too. That is, it can be quite poignant. For example, I was reading the newspaper the other day, and a headline caught my eye, as headlines are meant to do. It read "Lifeguard Drowns in Pool." While tragic, the irony is pretty obvious in that a professional lifesaver would drown in an everyday pool as compared to a riptide at the beach or something more dangerous. Of course, authors of literature are not always as direct with their irony, and we will sometimes read right over their intended meaning. Another example, perhaps more appropriate for this class, comes from Mark Twain's *The Adventures of Huckleberry Finn*. I believe you should be finished with this novel by our next class if I am not mistaken. In the novel, Twain uses situational irony throughout a greater part of the book as a kind of underlying theme of the story. Does anyone know what I'm speaking of . . . ? Nobody . . . ? That's okay. We'll get into it more once we start the novel, but it is an appropriate example related to irony which I'd like to touch on quickly. As many of you know, the theme of slavery is a major one in the novel. The main character, Huck Finn, is presented with an opportunity to help a runaway slave, which Huck considers a moral sin. Of course, the sin itself is the human bondage of slavery, which makes Huck's conflict ironic in a sense. Not helping a slave, the complete opposite, is the actual sin.

I'm not going to spoil the story for those of you who haven't read the novel yet, which, as far as I'm concerned, just doesn't seem possible considering its popularity and importance in American literature. Still, we'll come back to Huck's conflict when we begin the novel next week. Are there any questions at this point?

M: Isn't irony especially important in satire?

W: It sure is. Satirists almost always use irony in their work. For them, irony often represents the truth, that is, the message they are attempting to get across to the reader. An author's message will pervade the entire work, now and then implementing irony into its content. While irony can be humorous in every way, irony in a satire is simply a mechanism through which the author is able to reveal what she or he believes to be serious social or individual ills. Now, that's all I'm going to say on satire for the time being. **17** I know that I've assigned *Gulliver's Travels* for this semester, but why don't you guys add Swift's essay "A Modest Proposal" to your syllabus as well?

M: Oh, Professor Carter, thank you so much! You're so kind!

12 **Gist-Content Question**

Ⓒ The professor focuses on discusses irony in literature in the lecture.

13 **Detail Question**

Ⓑ The professor comments, "Well, irony in literature is typically defined as a verbal play on words or a situational expression different from or even completely the opposite of what the reader is expecting."

14 **Gist-Purpose Question**

Ⓒ The professor points out that irony is not always humorous in discussing the newspaper headline.

15 **Detail Question**

Ⓑ The professor states, "As many of you know, the theme of slavery is a major one in the novel. The main character, Huck Finn, is presented with an opportunity to help a runaway slave, which Huck considers a moral sin. Of course, the sin itself is the human bondage of slavery, which makes Huck's conflict ironic in a sense. Not helping a slave, the complete opposite, is the actual sin."

16 **Connecting Content Question**

Sarcasm: [1], [2] Irony: [3], [4]

About sarcasm, the professor states, "But sarcasm is usually more direct, bitter, biting, and obvious to the reader. As for irony, the professor notes, "Irony can be much more ambiguous and veiled," and then adds, "Satirists almost always use irony in their work."

17 **Understanding Function Question**

Ⓑ When the student says, "Oh, Professor Carter, thank you so much! You're so kind!" it can be inferred that he is being sarcastic about the extra work the professor just gave the class.

PART 2 Conversation 04-04   p.074

M Student: Hello. One of your cashiers told me to come and speak to you about returning books to the store. Are you Ms. Gibbons?

W Manager: Yes, I am Ms. Gibbons. You say that you need to return some books to the store? May I inquire as to the details, please?

M: Oh, sure. Well, here's the deal. You see, uh, I bought these books for my class . . . Economics 215 was the name of it. But I have to tell you that the class was absolutely horrid, so I dropped it.

W: That's Professor Bianconi's class, right?

M: How on Earth did you know that? What do you do, memorize the entire list of every class taught at this school?

W: Oh, goodness, no. I could never do that. I don't have the mental faculties for that. It's just that you are the fifth person to come in this morning to return books from his class. That must be some, uh, difficult, class if so many of you are dropping this late in the semester.

M: You have no idea . . . Anyway, he made us purchase three books for the class . . . Oh, you already know that, right?

W: I sure do. Here, let me take a look at them so that I can ascertain their condition and determine how much money you can get for them.

M: Here they are.

W: Hmm . . . This one here looks like it's in its original condition. I'm willing to bet that you only opened it once or twice. I can give you back the full price for this one, provided, of course, that you've brought your receipt with you. You did do that, didn't you?

M: Receipt? Oh, yeah, it's . . . uh, hold on a second . . . Yeah, I've got it. Here it is.

W: Let me take a look at it here . . . Wow, that's one long list of books you have there. I hope your parents paid for them and not you . . . Yes, here it is. I found it.

M: Great. That's the most expensive one. How about the other two books? Can I get back the full value for them as well?

W: Well, just by looking at the front cover of this book here, uh, *Principles of Macroeconomics* . . . I can tell you straight up that the most I can give you for that is fifty percent of its value. You shouldn't have written all over the front cover. It reduces the book's value.

M: **5** Yeah, but doodling on the book was a lot better than falling asleep in the middle of his lectures.

W: **Well, you may have a point.** Anyway, how does fifty percent sound for this book?

M: Sold! I just want it off my hands. And what do you think about the last one?

W: Well, it's in much better condition than some of the others I got today, but it's not quite in mint condition. Seventy-five percent is the most that I can give you.

M: Great. So how do I get my money back?

W: Leave the books with me and take this form up to the cashier. She'll either give you cash or credit your account. It's up to you.

1 Gist-Content Question
Ⓐ The speakers are mostly discussing the value of some books the student is returning.

2 Gist-Purpose Question
Ⓒ The student goes to the bookstore to return some books he does not need since he dropped a class.

3 Detail Question
Ⓒ The manager says, "You shouldn't have written all over the front cover. It reduces the book's value."

4 Understanding Attitude Question
Ⓑ The manager is very helpful to the student because she explains her reasoning.

5 Understanding Function Question
Ⓓ When the manager says, "Well, you may have a point," it can be inferred that she agrees with what the student told her.

PART 2 Lecture 🎧 04-05

M Professor: Many of us have a sweet tooth, don't we? Sugar and sugar substitutes are large parts of our diets from a very young age. The question is . . . which is better for us . . ? Is it one . . . or neither? With all the glucose and starch additives in foods these days, how do we know they aren't harming our bodies, uh, if not immediately, then in the long run. Obviously, diabetes is becoming more and more of a problem as people gain weight through the over-consumption of sugars, and their bodies are not able to break the sugar down. Enter sugar substitutes. Sugar substitutes have been around for quite a while. The first, original sugar substitute is called saccharin. That's S-A-C-C-H-A-R-I-N. Question?

W Student: Is this in our text, sir?

M: Well, there is a pretty good explanation of diabetes that I'd like you guys to take a look at tonight or before our next class because we are going to discuss it in more detail, but the sugar substitutes aren't in it, so be sure to take good notes on this stuff. It will definitely be on your midterm. Okay?

Again, the first sugar substitute, saccharin, was discovered way back in 1879. It is produced synthetically by combining certain compounds, and it is about three hundred times—yes, class, you heard me correctly— three hundred times sweeter than natural sugar. Even up until the 1970s, it was the only alternative to sugar out there. In addition, during this time, some of the first scientific studies were being done to test it to find out if it presented any health risks to the human body. **11** Actually, a few experiments on lab animals showed that the ones that ingested saccharin were more prone to certain types of cancer, which produced a big scare in countries such as the United States, which were, at the time, huge saccharin consumers. **But the FDA put those fears nearly to rest** by conducting its own experiments, which showed that people who used saccharin had no more risk of cancer than nonusers. The point is that virtually anything used in excess, be it food, drugs, alcohol, or whatever, can be harmful to the body. Moderation is key. Now, today both the FDA and AMA, that is, the Food and Drug Administration and the American Medical Association, both back saccharin as a sugar substitute in moderate quantities. Still, much of the public continues to be wary about it. Yes, question?

W: The little pink packets of Sweet'n Low contain saccharin, right?

M: Correct. And usually right next to them in a restaurant is the other major sugar substitute today, which contains the main ingredient called aspartame. That's A-S-P-A-R-T-A-M-E. Like saccharin, it is used in soft drinks and as a table sweetener, among other things. Aspartame is about two hundred times sweeter than sugar and is synthesized from various amino acids into a crystalline white powdery substance. Now, while the use of saccharin still raises an eyebrow with many people, the FDA claims that aspartame is completely safe and has been tested more than any other food additive for its safety and poses no threat to most people.

W: Why do you say most people, sir?

M: There is a general fear, especially in the U.S., over it because people think it causes diseases of the nervous system, certain forms of cancer, and even brain damage. According to the FDA, none of these risks exists whatsoever. The organization does concede, however, that aspartame can be dangerous to certain individuals. Let me explain.

Aspartame contains the amino acid phenylalanine, as do many other foods. Some people have a hereditary condition that does not allow them to metabolize this amino acid fast enough or even at all. In that way, it's much like how a lactose intolerant person has difficulty breaking down dairy products such as cheese and milk. The problem is more serious in the case of phenylalanine, especially with pregnant women, because the high levels of amino acids can build up and be passed on to the unborn child, thereby causing serious birth defects such as brain damage. Still, this is a rare condition in human beings, and for healthy individuals, neither the sugar substitute aspartame nor the amino acid phenylalanine is harmful at all. Let me reiterate this because it is a common misnomer about aspartame. It cannot cause serious health problems in individuals who do not suffer from the rare condition . . . Oh, it's called phenylketonuria. I'll write that on the board . . . There you go. Any questions?

W: What common sugar substitutes is aspartame in?

M: The brands NutraSweet and Equal contain aspartame, which, actually, I personally prefer over Sweet'n Low solely because of taste, not because I believe one is safer than the other. On the contrary, I firmly believe both are completely safe for most people.

6 Gist-Content Question

C The professor mostly discusses the characteristics of two sugar substitutes.

7 Detail Question

D The professor says, "The point is that virtually anything used in excess, be it food, drugs, alcohol, or whatever, can be harmful to the body. Moderation is key."

8 Detail Question

C The professor remarks, "The problem is more serious in the case of phenylalanine, especially with pregnant women, because the high levels of amino acids can build up and be passed on to the unborn child, thereby causing serious birth defects such as brain damage."

9 Connecting Content Question

Saccharin : 1, 4   Aspartame: 2, 3

About saccharin, the professor states, "Again, the first sugar substitute, saccharin, was discovered way back in 1879. It is produced synthetically by combining certain compounds, and it is about three hundred times—yes, class, you heard me correctly—three hundred times sweeter than natural sugar." As for aspartame, the professor says, "Aspartame contains the amino acid phenylalanine," and adds, "The brands NutraSweet and Equal contain aspartame."

10 Making Inferences Question

A The professor states, "The first sugar substitute, saccharin, was discovered way back in 1879." It can therefore be inferred that saccharin was created before aspartame, which is another sugar substitute.

11 Understanding Function Question

B In stating that people's fears were put "nearly to rest," the professor implies that the FDA could not get rid of the doubt in some people's minds.

ACTUAL TEST 05

p.081

Answers

PART 1

| 1 | C | 2 | B, C | 3 | A | 4 | C |
| 5 | D | 6 | A | 7 | C | 8 | D |

9 Tea Act: 1, 4   Intolerable Acts: 2, 3

10 B   11 B

PART 2

1	B	2	C	3	B	4	D
5	A	6	B	7	B	8	D
9	A, C	10	B	11	A	12	D
13	B	14	B, C				

15 Heat Exhaustion: 2, 3   Heatstroke: 1, 4

16 D   17 B

Scripts & Explanations

PART 1 Conversation 🎧 05-01   p.083

M Student Activities Office Employee: Hello. I believe you're next in line. What can I help you with today?

W Student: Good morning. Is this where I go to talk about clubs?

M: Well . . . Yes, but if you're looking to join a club, there was a big event which was held last week. Didn't you know about it?

W: Ah, actually, I attended it, but the club activity I am really interested in wasn't represented there. So I came here to ask about that particular club.

M: Which club do you want to join?

W: The cycling club. One of the seniors in my dormitory told me there's a cycling club on campus. Cycling is my favorite activity, so I thought I could try to do it with some like-minded people by joining the cycling club.

M: Hmm . . . I'm sorry, but we don't have a cycling club.

W: Do you mean she didn't tell the truth?

M: Not exactly. You see, we used to have a cycling club, um . . . two years ago. So your friend is probably remembering that. She just has outdated information.

W: What happened to the club?

M: If I remember correctly, it kind of disappeared due to a lack of interest. Two years ago, we had some really bad weather. There were a lot of storms, it snowed many times, including once in April, and temperatures were cold for most of the school year. As a result, few students ever went cycling. That pretty much caused the club to disappear the following year.

W: That's terrible. Is there, um, is there anything I can do about it?

M: [5] Sure. You could always start your own club.

W: Me? But I'm just a freshman.

M: **Don't sell yourself short**. Several of the clubs here were founded by first-year students, and many are quite successful.

W: Oh, uh, I wasn't aware of that. Is it hard to start a new club? I mean, um, I don't have the slightest clue how to do that.

M: No, it's not difficult at all. You simply fill out a form here that indicates your interest in starting a new club. Then, you can advertise in the school newspaper or online to let students know that a new club is being founded. After that, you have an initial meeting, during which you elect officers and decide how often the club is going to meet. Then, you conduct meetings throughout the semester. Well, in your case, I guess you would go riding at different places. It's really rather straightforward.

W: You make it sound so easy, but I'm not sure I'm up to the challenge.

M: Do you have a few minutes to spare right now? I can help you out with the process, but I also need to assist all of these other students who are waiting in line.

W: Actually, I have a class that begins in about fifteen minutes. How about if I return here at four o'clock?

M: That sounds perfect. Be here then. It will take me around twenty minutes to help you get started with everything.

W: Wonderful. I really appreciate your assistance. See you later in the day.

1 Gist-Content Question

Ⓒ The man tells the student, "I'm sorry, but we don't have a cycling club."

2 Detail Question

Ⓑ, Ⓒ The man says, "Two years ago, we had some really bad weather. There were a lot of storms, it snowed many times, including once in April, and temperatures were cold for most of the school year."

3 Understanding Attitude Question

Ⓐ When the student asks if starting a new club is difficult, the man responds, "No, it's not difficult at all."

4 Making Inference Question

Ⓒ The student comments, "Actually, I have a class that begins in about fifteen minutes."

5 Understanding Function Question

Ⓓ In stating, "Don't sell yourself short," the man is trying to encourage the student to start a new cycling club.

PART 1 Lecture 🎧 05-02   p.086

M Professor: As you know—well, at least you should know—our nation was founded in the late eighteenth century after a revolution against the British. There were thirteen colonies, all tied to Britain and answerable to the British monarch and Parliament. By the early 1770s, most Americans had been born here and had no personal ties to Britain. They saw themselves as Americans and were increasingly resentful of British interference in American affairs. As we already discussed, the early colonial period saw a great struggle between Britain and France for control of North America with the British finally winning after the end of the Seven Years' War in 1763. But this victory brought new problems, ones which eventually led to the American Revolution. The British passed a series of tax laws, or acts, which directly affected the American colonies and were the main cause of the revolution to come.

The war with France had cost the British a great deal of money, so they decided to begin taxing the Americans for the victory British arms had achieved for their benefit. [10] The British passed the, uh, Stamp Act in 1765. This stated that all documents, mostly legal documents such as wills and contracts, um, even newspapers and playing cards, had to carry a tax stamp. **It was strongly resisted by the colonists, and those individuals sent to collect the money were threatened with violence.** The act was done away with in 1766, but it aroused the suspicions of the colonists concerning British intentions.

Next were the Townsend Acts, named after Charles Townsend, the Chancellor of the Exchequer in Britain. He was like the country's chief financial officer. These were taxes set on certain things imported into the American colonies and again were designed to pay for the debt from the Seven Years' War. Once again, the colonists strongly resisted and began to organize themselves in protest groups. The colonists were also angry that they had no representatives in the British Parliament, where these acts were passed. This gave rise to the famous phrase "No taxation without representation."

[11] Then, the British passed the infamous Tea Act of 1773. This was designed to prop up the, uh, to support, the failing East India Company. The company was allowed to sell tea in the American colonies without paying the import tax others had to pay. This was supposed to make East India tea cheaper so that Americans would buy it. **Well, even the East India Company didn't make much money because most of the colonists boycotted tea.** This also led directly to the famous Boston Tea Party of December 16, 1773, which was when a group of American colonists threw a lot of crates of tea off three East India Company ships into Boston Harbor. Boston became one of the centers of the revolutionary cause.

But even before this, there had been violence in 1770. British soldiers had been stationed in many American cities, and Boston had one of the largest garrisons. The presence of the soldiers led to some incidents, of which the best-known one was the Boston Massacre of 1770. An altercation between civilians and soldiers on March 5, 1770, turned ugly when one soldier fired his weapon into a crowd, and others soon followed. Five men died, and eleven were wounded. It horrified the colonists, and the British soldiers were tried, but the trial concluded that the British soldiers had been threatened by the crowd and were justified in firing. Even so, passions were inflamed by the incident.

Then, between 1772 and 1775, a series of incidents led to the outbreak of war. I just mentioned the Boston Tea Party. In response to the colonists' resistance to tax laws, the British government passed a series of four laws that came to be—I mean, which the colonists called—the Intolerable Acts. These included the closing of Boston Harbor until the lost tea was paid for, um, which they, I mean, the colonists, never did. Another act that angered many was the Quartering Act, which was part of the Intolerable Acts. It meant that soldiers lived in civilians' houses with the owners responsible for their room and food. This quartering practice was one of the many grievances of the colonists, and the Constitution expressly forbids the quartering of soldiers on private citizens.

The other two Intolerable Acts restricted the government of Massachusetts from holding town meetings and stated that British soldiers would not be tried in the colonies but in Britain for offenses committed in the colonies. All this led to the eventual outbreak of fighting in April of 1775, when the British tried seizing arms the colonists were stockpiling. So we can conclude that the main causes of the revolution were the British attempts to tax the American colonists, the colonists' reaction to the tax laws, and the complications that arose from trying to enforce these acts.

6 Gist-Content Question

Ⓐ The professor focuses mainly on the grievances of the American colonists toward the British.

7 Detail Question

Ⓒ The professor says, "These were taxes set on certain things imported into the American colonies and again were designed to pay for the debt from the Seven Years' War."

8 Understanding Organization Question

Ⓓ The professor examines individual British acts and then discusses their effects.

9 Connecting Content Question

Tea Act: 1, 4   Intolerable Acts: 2, 3

About the Tea Act, the professor states, "This was designed to prop up the, uh, to support, the failing East India Company," and adds, "This also led directly to the famous Boston Tea Party of December 16, 1773, where a group of American colonists threw a lot of crates of tea off three East India Company ships into Boston Harbor." As for the Intolerable Acts, the professor remarks, "act that angered many was the Quartering Act, which was part of the Intolerable Acts," and also states, "Then, between 1772 and 1775, a series of incidents led to the outbreak of war."

10 Making Inferences Question

Ⓑ In stating, "It was strongly resisted by the colonists, and those individuals sent to collect the money were threatened with violence," the professor implies that very little money was collected by the tax collectors.

11 Understanding Function Question

Ⓑ In stating that most Americans boycotted tea, the professor is indicating that Americans refused to buy or drink tea.

PART 2 Conversation   🎧 05-03   p.089

W Student: Professor Dawkins, could you spare a couple of minutes? I have some questions for you.

M Professor: Sure, sure. Please come in. I happen to be having office hours right now, so I'm all yours until four o'clock.

W: Oh, goodness. I don't think my questions are going to take that long. Anyway, I have some questions about our class syllabus if you don't mind.

M: Of course not. What's bothering you about it?

W: Well, first off . . . I noticed that there are nine books listed on the syllabus. Nine! Surely that must be a misprint of some kind. I don't think I could read nine books in a year.

M: Well, I'm sorry to disappoint you, but you're going to have to learn to read a little more quickly than you're used to. But don't worry too much about that. I get students every semester . . . you're the third today in fact . . . telling me how there is no way that they'll be able to handle the workload.

W: And, uh, how do they, uh, usually wind up doing in your class?

M: Not well at all, I'm afraid . . . Oh, don't look so worried. I'm just having a little fun with you. Actually, in every one of those instances, my students have acquitted themselves rather nicely, and in some cases, they proved to be the best students in the class.

W: Well, that's a relief to hear. I guess that should give me some confidence.

M: As well it should. You're a freshman, aren't you?

W: Yes, sir.

M: That's what I thought. Remember that college is a lot more rigorous than what you're used to. You probably read, uh, what, maybe two books a year in your high school lit classes, right? Well, we're a lot more intense here, so we'll be doing a minimum of one book every two weeks. Now, now, get that scared look off of your face. You can do it. Really. I guarantee that you'll find a way to get through all these books, understand them, and, most importantly, enjoy them.

W: ⁴Well, I sure hope so. I've always wanted to study nineteenth-century British literature, and this is a great chance. **I just hope that I haven't bitten off more than I can chew.**

M: Look . . . You got good grades in high school, right? Otherwise, you wouldn't be at this school. So it's clear that you can do the work. You'll just have to find ways to, you know, make the most of your time. You probably weren't anywhere nearly as efficient a worker as you could have been in high school. Well, now's the time to start learning to apply yourself.

W: You know . . . you're right, sir. I really didn't make the most of my time last year. I guess I'll have to teach myself how to do it.

M: You sure will because I'm not the easiest grader in the world. If your work starts to lag behind the others, I'll be sure to let you know . . . in the form of a bad grade on your test or paper.

W: ⁵Uh, yes, sir. I think I see your point. I'm going to head home now and get to work on our first book.

M: **That's the spirit.**

1 Gist-Purpose Question

Ⓑ The student visits to ask about one of the course requirements.

2 Detail Question

ⓒ The professor remarks, "Actually, in every one of those instances, my students have acquitted themselves rather nicely, and in some cases, they proved to be the best students in the class."

3 Making Inferences Question

ⓑ In stating, "Remember that college is a lot more rigorous than what you're used to. You probably read, uh, what, maybe two books a year in your high school lit classes, right? Well, we're a lot more intense here," the professor implies that the student's high school was not as rigorous as the college she is attending.

4 Understanding Attitude Question

ⓓ In stating, "I just hope that I haven't bitten off more than I can chew," the student means that she does not know if she can handle the class.

5 Understanding Function Question

ⓐ In stating, "That's the spirit," the professor is showing that he is pleased with the student's comment.

PART 2 Lecture #1   🎧 05-04   p.092

W Professor: One of the common features of almost every animal on our planet is eyes. Yet not all eyes are the same. Some eyes are better at seeing than others, some are more color sensitive, and some have great night vision whereas some animals hardly use their eyes at all. Some eyes are small and cute, and others are large and frightening. So today I want to talk about, uh, the main types of eyes and how they have developed to enable animals to use them.

¹⁰ Now just one thing before I begin. Excuse me . . . I will be speaking in generalities. This means that while I will make a statement concerning eyes, **I'm sure everyone, uh, or at least some of you, will think of an example that contradicts what I say.** Just remember this . . . There are no absolutes in the animal kingdom. Even now we are finding more species, and sometimes they don't fit into one of our neat little areas of classification. Okay?

There are two main types of eyes: directional and image forming. Directional eyes only sense light and belong to a whole range of small creatures, such as worms. They use light to know where they are going. For most of these creatures, there is no need to form images since they live underground. Now, image-forming eyes are what are found in most other creatures on the Earth, including humans. Almost all vertebrates, uh, animals with spines or backbones, have image-forming eyes. It means we see things by taking the light from them and projecting it onto a retina, which then transmits an image to the brain. Not all creatures see the same image.

Color is important. Humans have perhaps the most color-sensitive eyes. Our retinas have 125 million thin, straight rods that can see black and white and seven million rods that see color. We are attracted to certain colors, and other colors can make us have different emotions. For example, blue is a calming color while red causes increased blood pressure and sometimes anger. Some people and animals are colorblind. Colorblindness means someone, or an animal, has trouble distinguishing between certain colors, often green and brown, blue and purple, or yellow and orange. While we have done some studies on animal color sensitivity, it is difficult to study animal vision because we can't determine how they form images and what colors they see.

Now let me talk about how eyes are positioned on the head. The position of the eyes on the head relates to how an animal gets its food. The two most common positions are looking forward, or binocular vision, and then there are those animals with sideways vision, so they have their eyes on either side of their heads. Predators, hunters I mean, have binocular vision because they need to look forward at their prey while attacking it. The members of the cat family are perfect examples of predators with eyes designed for hunting. They can see in a 287-degree arc, and their eyes are highly adapted to the dark. Some animals, such as hunting birds like hawks, have excellent long-range vision used for hunting. A hawk can spot a rabbit in a field from up to a mile away, swoop in, and strike its prey very quickly before the rabbit can bound away.

Most herbivores, you know, uh, plant eaters, have eyes on each side of their heads, so they can see to the left, to the right, and behind them, where predators are most likely to come from. For example, deer, elk, giraffes, and a multitude of others have this sideway vision from having to avoid hunters, a constant pressure in their lives.

Other eyes are used to scare away danger. For example, the eyes of baboons get large, brighten, and make direct eye contact to scare away enemies. If this doesn't work, they bare their very long teeth. The eyes of a panda are small but are in a patch of black hair, which makes then seem larger and more threatening. Ironically, this black patch makes pandas seem cute to humans. Our nature is conditioned to adore and love what is called the typical infant's face—you know, big eyes, a flat face, and the snub nose of an infant. Perhaps this emotion was developed so that mothers would not abandon their children. Anyway, you can see influences of this in Japanese animation, where all the characters have unusually big eyes that are often brimming with emotion.

Okay. I got a little off track there. Sorry. Finally, other animal's eyes are not very good at vision. They have eyes, but they have limited functions. Bats have poor vision and use echoes to find their way at night. [11] Elephants can't see much after a few dozen yards. This makes them dangerous because they can smell and sense an unknown presence and may charge. **Elephants are often feared more by people than any snake, lion, or tiger.**

6 Gist-Content Question

Ⓑ The professor mostly talks about the types of purposes of animals' eyes.

7 Understanding Organization Question

Ⓑ The professor states, "Directional eyes only sense light and belong to a whole range of small creatures, such as worms."

8 Detail Question

Ⓓ The professor says, "While we have done some studies on animal color sensitivity, it is difficult to study animal vision because we can't determine how they form images and what colors they see."

9 Detail Question

Ⓐ, Ⓒ The professor tells the students, "For example, the eyes of baboons get large, brighten, and make direct eye contact to scare away enemies."

10 Understanding Attitude Question

Ⓑ In stating, "I'm sure everyone, uh, or at least some of you, will think of an example that contradicts what I say," the professor means that the students will think of a case that does not fit what she just said.

11 Understanding Attitude Question

Ⓐ In stating, "Elephants are often feared more by people than any snake, lion, or tiger," the professor implies that elephants kill people at times.

PART 2 Lecture #2 🎧 05-05   p.095

W Professor: Dehydration can be quite dangerous. It occurs when the body loses more fluids than it takes in. Remember that we humans need at least a liter of water every day. But this is a very conservative measurement. Depending on how active you are, you may require five or even ten times this amount. Most health specialists suggest we drink water even if we are not thirsty. This is especially important in dry climates.

Now, a number of factors cause general dehydration. The most obvious is increased activity from work or exercise, particularly outdoors in the sun. When we sweat, we lose fluids. If we don't replenish them, we become prone to dehydration. But there are other causes as well. Fever is one. When we are sick, our bodies use more fluids than normal to cool them and to fight off diseases. Intestinal viruses and other problems with the, uh, digestive system cause dehydration, too. [17] **Sometimes even though we drink fluids, they exit our system before the body can absorb them.** Nausea, vomiting, and, um, diarrhea are common causes of dehydration as well. Now, are there, um, any questions at this point, class?

M Student: Isn't dehydration a common symptom of heat-related illnesses? I think I read that somewhere.

W: You're absolutely right. Heat-related illnesses occur when the body has trouble cooling itself. One reason for this problem is the lack of fluids in the body, you know, a dehydrated body. It might sound like a cliché, class, but water is life. It is absolutely essential for the body to function properly.

Let's take the example of outdoor exercise again. Now, of course, a really hot day will increase our chances of dehydration and heat-related illnesses. But couple a hot day with high humidity, and the risk increases even more. That's right. This increased risk is due to the fact that even though the body is able to sweat, high humidity traps sweat on the skin. It cannot evaporate fast enough and, in turn, traps heat more and more inside the body. Even though the body is trying to cool itself down, the high humidity really makes it work against itself. Yes, you have another question?

M: What about low humidity environments, Professor Perkins?

W: That's a good question. If humidity is low and the air temperature is hot, our bodies will still sweat to cool themselves. The difference is, uh, many times in low humidity, we don't know we're sweating. Sweat evaporates that quickly from our skin. This can be dangerous too because we might not feel as thirsty as we really are. In hot, dry climates, the need to drink fluids constantly is even more prevalent.

There are basically two kinds of heat-related illnesses: heat exhaustion and heatstroke. Heat exhaustion is really just extreme dehydration, uh, when the body loses too many fluids and too much salt. It typically happens from excessive work or exercise outdoors in hot weather. In such an environment, if the individual doesn't continually replace these fluids and salts by drinking enough water, he could become vulnerable to heat exhaustion. Don't let the name fool you because heat exhaustion can be quite dangerous—even life threatening. One of the reasons it is so dangerous is that it develops very slowly and gradually. Some of the more common symptoms associated with heat exhaustion are excessive sweating, fatigue, headaches, dizziness, and fainting. A person suffering from heat exhaustion will also have a rapid but weak pulse, and that person's breathing will be rapid and short. Heat exhaustion is fairly easy to counteract. The individual should relocate to a cool area and rest while drinking a lot of fluids. If the person is unable to keep fluids down, he should visit the hospital for an IV.

M: I'm sorry if this sounds stupid, ma'am, but what exactly is in an IV in this situation?

W: It's not a stupid question at all. In the case of heat exhaustion, the IV will probably be a type of electrolyte saline solution that the doctor will slowly feed directly into your bloodstream. This will quickly rehydrate the body.

The second type is more serious: heatstroke. This occurs when the body's cooling system completely shuts down and cannot function. Heatstroke can develop very quickly and really seem to come out of nowhere. Like heat exhaustion, it can happen from overexertion or exercise, but medications, especially high blood pressure medicine, can also cause heatstroke. Symptoms include a fast, strong pulse, confusion, very little or no sweat at all, hot, red skin, and in the most extreme cases, convulsions and hyperventilation. If you suspect someone is suffering from heatstroke, you must take that person to the hospital or call an ambulance as fast as possible. Doctors will then attempt to lower the body's core temperature.

12 Gist-Content Question

Ⓓ The lecture is mostly about the causes and effects of heat-related illnesses.

13 Detail Question

Ⓑ The professor lectures, "Dehydration can be quite dangerous. It occurs when the body loses more fluids than it takes in."

14 Detail Question

Ⓑ, Ⓒ The professor states, "Some of the more common symptoms associated with heat exhaustion are excessive sweating, fatigue, headaches, dizziness, and fainting."

15 Connecting Content Question

Heat Exhaustion: ②, ③   Heatstroke: ①, ④

About heat exhaustion, the professor notes, "Some of the more common symptoms associated with heat exhaustion are excessive sweating, fatigue, headache, dizziness, and fainting," and adds, "A person suffering from heat exhaustion will also have a rapid but weak pulse." As for heatstroke, the professor states, "Symptoms include a fast, strong pulse, confusion, very little or no sweat at all, hot, red skin, and in the most extreme cases, convulsions and hyperventilation."

16 Making Inferences Question

Ⓓ When the professor says, "The second type is more serious: heatstroke," she implies that heat exhaustion is less dangerous than heatstroke.

17 Understanding Function Question

Ⓑ In stating, "Sometimes even though we drink fluids, they exit our system before the body can absorb them," the professor implies that drinking fluids does not always help.

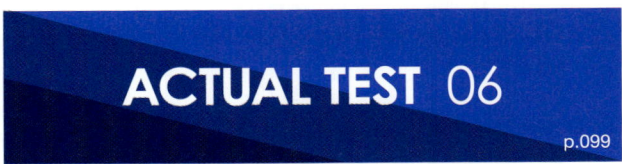

ACTUAL TEST 06

Answers

PART 1

1	Ⓑ	2	Ⓑ	3	Ⓓ	4	Ⓐ, Ⓓ
5	Ⓑ	6	Ⓑ	7	Ⓑ	8	Ⓒ
9	Ⓑ	10 Toucan: ①, ④ Quetzal: ②, ③
11	Ⓐ

PART 2

| 1 | Ⓒ | 2 | Ⓓ | 3 | Ⓑ | 4 | Ⓒ |
| 5 | Ⓑ | 6 | Ⓓ | 7 | Ⓒ | 8 | Ⓑ |
| 9 Monopoly: ②, ④   Oligopoly: ①, ③ |
10	Ⓐ	11	Ⓐ	12	Ⓒ	13	Ⓒ
14	Ⓓ	15 Sympathetic Nervous System: ②, ③ Limbic System: ①, ④
16	Ⓑ	17	Ⓐ

Scripts & Explanations

PART 1 Conversation 🎧 06-01

M Professor: Oh, hi. Thanks a lot for coming. I know you are capable of getting a good score in this class, Denise. It is just that your test and quiz scores aren't reflecting your potential. Here's your most recent test. Take a look.

W Student: A C minus? I studied for days for this one. I thought I would at least get a B on it.

M: I really don't understand. You always come to class, and your comments in class are excellent.

W: Well, I don't know either, sir. Maybe it is my part-time job.

M: Do you really think it is affecting your work? Because if it is, you should probably cut back on your hours or possibly even quit it.

W: No, I only work like, uh, eight hours a week. I have plenty of time for studying. I told you that I studied for like three days straight for this exam.

M: Okay. Okay. Try to calm down. We'll work this out one way or another. What about your study methods? Explain to me how you prepare for the exams.

W: I usually go over my notes from class over and over again.

M: Do you just read them or write them down?

W: I read them.

M: Well, I suggest you outline your notes on a separate sheet of paper or something. You'll remember them better, and having that kind of organization will help you considerably with the essay section of the test. Many times, your ideas are correct, but there is no structure with regard to how you present them in essay form.

W: Okay. I'll try that next time. Thanks.

M: I would also suggest going to the writing lab. I really believe your main problem is your essays. You really need someone to guide you and help you structure and organize your essays better. These tests during the semester have some multiple-choice questions, which are, to be frank, saving your grade. The final does not. It is all essays. So you must get this taken care of before then.

W: Okay. I'll make an appointment at the writing lab.

M: Don't make an appointment. Just go there. The sooner you start, the sooner your grades will begin to improve not only in my class but your others as well.

W: I get your point. Do you have any other advice for me?

M: Why don't you talk to Angela Bingham? Do you know who she is?

W: Yes. She sits in the front all the time, right?

M: Yes, she does. She's a senior and is the leader of a study group for the class. You might want to ask her if you can join her group. The students in the group can give you some other tips on studying and the subject.

W: Okay. I'll talk to her next class. I bet she can help me out.

M: Great. Now, I've got my own lecture in about one minute, so I have to run. If there isn't anything else, I'll see you later. I hope my advice helps you out.

W: Okay. Thanks, sir.

1 Gist-Content Question

Ⓑ The speakers are mostly talking about why the student does poorly in the professor's class.

2 Gist-Purpose Question

Ⓑ The professor says, "It is just that your test and quiz scores aren't reflecting your potential. Here's your most recent test."

3 Detail Question

Ⓓ The professor states, "I really believe your main problem is your essays. You really need someone to guide you and help you structure and organize your essays better."

4 Detail Question

Ⓐ, Ⓓ The professor tells the student, "Well, I suggest you outline your notes on a separate sheet of paper or something. You'll remember them better, and having that kind of organization will help you considerably with the essay section of the test," and adds, "Yes, she does. She's a senior and is the leader of a study group for the class. You might want to ask her if you can join her group."

5 Making Inferences Question

Ⓑ The professor tells the student, "Don't make an appointment. Just go there. The sooner you start, the sooner your grades will begin to improve not only in my class but your others as well," so she will probably go to the writing lab next.

PART 1 Lecture   p.104

M Professor: We know from our lecture last week that the world's rainforests hold an impressive assortment of wildlife. Their ecosystems teem with curious creatures not found anywhere else. What I want to do now is explore some of these animals a little more closely. I thought we would start in the canopy of the rainforest today, class, and eventually work our way down to the ground level and beyond. Probably one of the most famous and visible birds of the South American rainforests is the *Ramphastos sulfuratos*. Oh, no one recognizes this name? Well, you should because it is the scientific name for the toucan.

W Student: Oh, yes, Professor Kelvin. That's that colorful bird with the big beak.

M: Actually, the more appropriate term for it is a bill. While they primarily serve the same purpose, bills are usually larger than beaks. Beaks are for smaller birds and are not as elongated. Still, you are correct. It has a very large bill and is quite colorful, and the toucan is perhaps one of the most exotic and recognizable birds in the world. Here . . . I brought some photos of my trip to Venezuela. Everyone, take a look up at the screen. The average size of a toucan is about one and a half feet in length, and here . . . you can see that huge rainbow-colored bill. The bill itself is about a third of the toucan's body. Question?

W: Is there any special reason for its gigantic size?

M: Good question. Scientists still are not sure. Some propose the toucan uses it to pluck large fruit from trees. You see, the toucan mainly feeds on different types of fruit in the rainforest, but it doesn't chew the fruit. It actually swallows it whole, and it is likely that its large bill is necessary for this type of feeding.

In addition, of course, it is excellent camouflage for the toucan in the trees of the rainforest, so the bill protects the toucan from predators. The toucan's diet is not limited to fruit though. It occasionally feeds on insects, small reptiles, and amphibians. **11** There's another interesting note to the toucan's fruity diet. The fruit trees that it feeds on rely on the toucan as well as the other birds of the rainforest for their own seed dispersion. **In many ways, it is a two-way street.** That is, they really rely on each other for survival. The toucan spits out the seeds or releases them in its dung, and seedlings later sprout from the seeds on the fertile floor of the rainforest. Pretty neat, isn't it?

Another curious point about the toucan is that it is terrible at flying. It is able to fly some, but its main form of locomotion is actually jumping. Toucans live together in small groups and usually travel by jumping from limb to limb and from tree to tree in the canopy. Yes, question?

W: Um, what about their homes? I mean nests, right?

M: They do not actually build nests out of sticks and twigs on tree limbs. Instead, they nest inside trees in cavities and old holes made by other animals. Remember that the rainforest receives a lot of rain, class, and I mean a lot. Nesting inside trees instead of in an open nest gives the toucan more protection from the often nasty weather of the rainforest.

Now, if there are no more questions, let's move on to another exotic bird of the rainforests. It's called the quetzal. It lives in the rainforests of both Central and South America unlike the toucan, which lives only in South America. Many consider the quetzal one of the most beautiful birds in the entire world because it is a brilliant metallic green color and has long tail feathers that extend two or even three feet in length. Like the toucan, it is a poor flyer, but it is a solitary bird, so it likes to live by itself. Another interesting fact is that it cannot survive in captivity. No one really knows why this is, but you can only see the quetzal in the wild, not at zoos or bird sanctuaries. The habitat of the quetzal is also unique because it lives in what we call cloud forests. These forests exist in the upper elevations of mountains in rainforests, and it usually lives at about the five-thousand-foot region on up to about ten thousand feet, and much like the toucan, it lives in hollow cavities in trees. The difference is the quetzal lives much higher up in the tree. It can sometimes be found fifty to sixty feet from ground level. This gives it better protection from predators. In addition, similar to the toucan, the quetzal is an integral player in the dispersion of the seeds of the trees. It feeds on fruit and disperses seeds on the floor of the forest.

6   Gist-Content Question

Ⓑ The professor mainly discusses exotic birds in the rainforests of the Americas.

7   Understanding Organization Question

Ⓑ The professor stays, "Some propose the toucan uses it to pluck large fruit from trees. You see, the toucan mainly feeds on different types of fruit in the rainforest, but it doesn't chew the fruit. It actually swallows it whole, and it is likely that its large bill is necessary for this type of feeding."

8   Detail Question

Ⓒ The professor says, "They do not actually build nests out of sticks and twigs on tree limbs. Instead, they nest inside trees in cavities and old holes made by other animals."

9   Detail Question

Ⓑ The professor states, "Another interesting fact is that it cannot survive in captivity."

10   Connecting Content Question

Toucan: 1, 4   Quetzal: 2, 3

About the toucan, the professor says, "Unlike the toucan, which lives only in South America," and adds, "Toucans live together in small groups and usually travel by jumping from limb to limb and from tree to tree in the canopy." As for the quetzal, the professor notes, "Many consider the quetzal one of the most beautiful birds in the entire world because it is a brilliant metallic green color and has long tail feathers that extend two or even three feet in length," and, "These forests exist in the upper elevations of mountains in rainforests, and it usually lives at about the five-thousand-foot region on up to about ten thousand feet."

11 Understanding Function Question

Ⓐ In stating, "In many ways, it is a two-way street," the professor implies that the toucan and its sources of food depend on each other.

PART 2 Conversation 06-03   p.107

W Student: Is this where I can pick up some scholarship applications?

M Employee: It sure is. What type do you want to apply for?

W: I'm not sure. I'm a sophomore. What types are available for me?

M: That depends. Each scholarship has a different type of criteria you must meet in order to qualify for it.

W: Oh, I see.

M: How is your GPA? And are you involved in any of the different student organizations?

W: Well, my GPA is about a 3.8. I'm also in two academic honors societies, and I am the president of the anthropological society on campus.

M: Wow. That's pretty impressive. With credentials like that, you probably won't have any trouble qualifying for any number of scholarships. Personally, I think you should apply for the Wells Scholarship.

W: Really? Why?

M: For one thing, it pays for your entire tuition until you graduate. I mean, even if you graduate late or take longer than expected to graduate, it will pay for your classes and all your textbooks.

W: Really? That sounds excellent.

M: Can I ask you a kind of personal question?

W: Go ahead.

M: You are a sophomore, right? Why did you wait so long to apply for scholarships? Most students do so before they ever set foot on campus as a freshman.

W: I just transferred here last semester. I didn't think my former college was challenging enough, so I decided to make a change and come here. I'm much happier here because the courses are more diverse than what I was used to.

M: Aha . . . I see. Well, there's one other thing that I forgot to mention to you about the Wells Scholarship. I believe the deadline for it is this Friday. That only gives you about three days to complete it and to write and polish your essay.

W: Essay? I didn't know that scholarship applications required an essay.

M: Sure. Most, but not all, of them do. Actually, with the Wells, the scholarship puts more weight on the personal essay than any other element of your application. It is even more important than your GPA because it provides the people who decide on the recipient with more insight into your individual character and goals.

W: I guess that makes sense. Do you know how long it must be?

M: I believe it is three typed pages. Oh, I just thought of something else. You need your official transcripts for the application. That means you must get your former college to send them as quickly as possible to me. That means now. Here's the address.

W: Thanks! Wow, you are really helpful! I really appreciate it!

M: There's one more thing. The application fee is one hundred dollars. I know it seems like a lot, but it really is worth it considering what you can gain from the scholarship.

W: That's not a problem. I just need to get on that essay and my transcript. Once I finish, I just come back and turn everything in to you?

M: Yes, that would be best since you're running out of time.

1 Gist-Content Question

Ⓒ The speakers are mostly discussing applying for a scholarship.

2 Gist-Purpose Question

Ⓓ At the beginning of the conversation, the student says, "Is this where I can pick up some scholarship applications?"

3 Detail Question

Ⓑ The man says, "For one thing, it pays for your entire tuition until you graduate. I mean, even if you graduate late or take longer than expected to graduate, it will pay for your classes and all your textbooks."

4 Detail Question

Ⓒ The man tells the student, "Actually, with the Wells, the scholarship puts more weight on the personal essay than any other element of your application."

5 Making Inferences Question

Ⓑ The student says, "I just need to get on that essay and my transcript," while the man adds, "That means you must get your former college to send them as quickly as possible to me. That means now. Here's the address."

PART 2 Lecture #1 🎧 06-04   p.110

W Professor: There are a number of types of domination by companies in the market. Probably the best-known kind is the, er, monopoly. There are many different kinds of monopolies, but in general, one exists when a company or firm supplies a good or service to consumers and basically has little or no competition in the market. Monopolies can exist at every level. They can exist locally all the way up to internationally. Who can give me an example of a local monopoly?

M Student: How about if a small town only has one drugstore?

W: Sure. That's an excellent example. The market is the town itself, and it has no direct competition in that market. If you need a prescription filled, you have no choice but to go to the one place that provides that product. How about at the regional level? Any ideas for an example of a monopoly at the regional level, class?

M: Let me see . . . What about something like a power company?

W: Well done. How many of you live in a private apartment? Let me see a show of hands. Okay. I would say just over half of you. Well, what about when you moved in? You had to get your electricity hooked up, right? [11] Did you have a choice? Not really. In most regions, there is only one provider for that area. Again, this is another example of a monopoly. **If you don't want to use the electric company's services, you'd better get the candles ready.** Actually, utility companies are one of the most common monopolies in the world today.

　Let's move on to an example of a national monopoly. In the U.S., these used to be more common than they are now. Nowadays, the government intervenes if a company dominates the national market in most cases. But we'll get into more detail on government intervention in a bit. Ideas?

M: Um, well, what about, uh, you know, phone companies? I know a long time ago that the only way to call people in other states was through AT&T. People had no choice. It was the only company controlling long distance calls.

W: You are exactly right, and that is an excellent example. Yes, the U.S. government found that AT&T did monopolize the long-distance telephone market, deemed it illegal, and eventually split the company up. Today, monopolies such as that one are illegal in the U.S. Yes, question?

M: But why do they or how are they able to exist in the first place?

W: Usually, it is due to what we economists call an entry barrier. Something will not allow other companies to enter a given market in order to compete with an existing company. Often, the monopolizing company is the only one that has access to a certain resource, like our utility example, of water, electricity, or technology. So another point about monopolies is that they usually have little or no competition from competitors, which means they do not really need to reduce the prices of their goods and services. Of course, they cannot simply charge whatever they want due to the law of demand. Still, they can often charge a premium because they are the only providers of certain things.

　They also use another tactic for their benefit called price discrimination. This means they can charge different prices to different consumers to maximize and increase their profits. A good example of price discrimination is the airline industry. Oh, let me make a quick point about the airline industry before I move on. In essence, it is what we call an oligopoly. It used to be more prevalent before the nineties in the U.S., when only a few carriers ruled the skies. Today, with deregulation, there are many more airlines to choose from. Still, many monopolize certain regions of the country as well as international routes. The difference between an oligopoly and a monopoly is that when there's an oligopoly, a group of companies works in unison to control prices and sales in their given industry. In addition, especially today, oligopolies are much more common than true monopolies.

　Now, let's get back to price discrimination. Think about it, class. Economy-class tickets and cheap seats go in general to certain consumers as do business-class and first-class seats. In reality, it is virtually the same service: The airlines transport people from point A to point B with different or no perks at all. This way, airlines can maximize their profits by charging certain consumers certain prices. It becomes more complex when you add in advance purchases, discounts, and senior citizen or student tickets. Airlines are also able to regulate it all by imposing strict rules on refunds and the reissuing of tickets. Once a ticket is sold, it cannot be transferred to another person, which adds to the airline protecting its profits.

6　Gist-Content Question

　Ⓓ　The professor mostly discusses different types of monopolies.

7　Detail Question

　Ⓒ　The professor says, "Yes, the U.S. government found that AT&T did monopolize the long-distance telephone market, deemed it illegal, and eventually split the company up."

8 **Detail Question**

   Ⓑ The professor says, "This way, airlines can maximize their profits by charging certain consumers certain prices."

9 **Connecting Content Question**

   Monopoly: ②, ④   Oligopoly: ①, ③

   About monopolies, the professor states, "In general, one exists when a company or firm supplies a good or service to consumers and basically has little or no competition in the market," and adds, "Actually, utility companies are one of the most common monopolies in the world today." As for oligopolies, the professor notes, "The difference between an oligopoly and a monopoly is that when there's an oligopoly, a group of companies works in unison to control prices and sales in their given industry," and, "Oh, let me make a quick point about the airline industry before I move on. In essence, it is what we call an oligopoly."

10 **Making Inferences Question**

   Ⓐ When the professor states, "Still, they can often charge a premium because they are the only providers of certain things," it can be inferred that more competition would lower prices.

11 **Understanding Function Question**

   Ⓐ In stating, "If you don't want to use the electric company's services, you'd better get the candles ready," the professor implies that people will not have power.

PART 2 Lecture #2 🎧 06-05   p.113

M Professor: Could someone turn off the lights, please? I want to use my laptop for this part of the presentation and show you a few things. As you can see from the diagram on the screen, the areas highlighted in blue are major parts of the body that control your nervous system and your emotions. Everything from fear to anger to sadness to depression probably comes from one of these areas or systems. First of all, I want to talk about the autonomic nervous system, also known as the ANS. As you can probably gather from its name, it runs automatically, or what we would call involuntarily. ¹⁶ While we do have some control over it, for the most part, it is a kind of defense mechanism when we experience extreme situations. BOO! I scared some of you, didn't I?

W Student: Professor Martin, you almost gave me a heart attack. My heart is racing!

M: That's exactly the affect I was looking for. It is also a perfect example of your ANS at work. Actually, the ANS consists of two main parts: the sympathetic nervous system and the parasympathetic nervous system, which work together in situations like this. When I scared some of you, your sympathetic nervous system took over. This caused you to jump to attention and to get ready for action. In essence, it is your inner defense mechanism. This is what alerts your body and emotions to potential dangers. It actually governs your fight or flight mechanism. That is, you ask, "Should I stay, engage the situation, and fight, or is it too dangerous, so should I flee?"

Whatever option you choose, your body's sympathetic nervous system readies your body instantaneously into its optimum condition for reaction or action. Your heart rate immediately increases, pumping more oxygen to the tissues of your body, especially your muscles. Your sweat glands open up and are ready to cool your body down if needed. Your blood vessels expand, and your pupils dilate for better vision. All of this happens in a split second thanks to your sympathetic nervous system. More specifically, the sympathetic nervous system regulates the adrenal glands. These are the glands that produce adrenaline. Actually, in our bodies, we call it epinephrine. Doctors concoct adrenaline from epinephrine for medical procedures. Epinephrine is an amazing hormone the body uses in times of emergency or high stress situations. This quick jolt of epinephrine gives you extra strength and endurance.

¹⁷ I'm sure many of you have seen some of the amazing human stories where some guy lifts a car in an accident to save his wife or child or something. **Well, it probably did occur just as they say it did because the body is capable of such amazing feats when its back is up against a wall.** Pretty impressive, huh? Of course, it is only possible thanks to the ANS and the sympathetic nervous system. Now the reciprocal of the sympathetic nervous system is the parasympathetic nervous system. This is in charge of calming your body back down to a normal state after the danger passes and the coast is clear. It reduces your heart rate, slows your breathing, shuts down the adrenal gland, and calms the sweat glands. In the science world, we call this homeostasis. This is the ability for humans as well as organisms to maintain a balance or, uh, equilibrium, both physically as well as emotionally. I mean, think about it, class. Different stimuli affect our bodies with every moment. The ANS is constantly monitoring and managing the levels of our emotions to keep everything even and normal. This is the primary function of the different nervous systems of our bodies. Yes, question?

W: But what about the brain, Professor Martin?

M: Okay. Could someone please turn on the lights? Thank you. Now, the brain is next on the agenda today. Our brains house the limbic system. The limbic system also plays an important role in regulating emotions. It is at the base of the brain near the brain's cortex. It has three main parts: the hypothalamus, the hippocampus, and the amygdala.

Let's explore the hypothalamus first. It is a highly active part of the brain and typically controls or monitors sensations such as fatigue, hunger, and thirst. It receives the information from certain organs and areas via nerves and then creates the necessary sensation. Some experts also believe that the hypothalamus is also responsible for certain emotions such as anger and sadness. It is possible that the limbic system works in conjunction with the ANS in certain situations as well. That is, the limbic system alerts the ANS to heighten the physical responses of our bodies.

12 Gist-Content Question

Ⓒ The professor mostly lectures about the function of the sympathetic nervous system.

13 Detail Question

Ⓒ The professor says, "When I scared some of you, your sympathetic nervous system took over. This caused you to jump to attention and to get ready for action. In essence, it is your inner defense mechanism. This is what alerts your body and emotions to potential dangers."

14 Detail Question

Ⓓ The professor remarks, "In the science world, we call this homeostasis. This is the ability for humans as well as organisms to maintain a balance or, uh, equilibrium, both physically as well as emotionally."

15 Connecting Content Question

Sympathetic Nervous System: ②, ③ Limbic System: ①, ④
About the sympathetic nervous system, the professor states, "Your heart rate immediately increases, pumping more oxygen to the tissues of your body, especially your muscles," and adds, "More specifically, the sympathetic nervous system regulates the adrenal glands. These are the glands that produce adrenaline." As for the limbic system, the professor notes, "The limbic system also plays an important role in regulating emotions. It is at the base of the brain near the brain's cortex. It has three main parts: the hypothalamus, the hippocampus, and the amygdala," and, "It is a highly active part of the brain and typically controls or monitors sensations such as fatigue, hunger, and thirst."

16 Understanding Attitude Question

Ⓑ When the student says, "Professor Martin, you almost gave me a heart attack," it can be inferred that the student is scared.

17 Understanding Function Question

Ⓐ In stating, "Well, it probably did occur just as they say it did because the body is capable of such amazing feats when its back is up against a wall," the professor implies that people can do things they normally cannot during difficult circumstances.

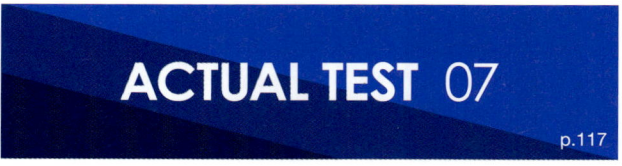

ACTUAL TEST 07

p.117

Answers

PART 1

1 Ⓑ	2 Ⓐ	3 Ⓒ,Ⓓ	4 Ⓐ
5 Ⓓ	6 Ⓑ	7 Ⓐ	8 Ⓐ,Ⓓ
9 Ⓓ	10 Ⓑ		

11 Oases: ② Wells: ①, ③, ④

PART 2

| 1 Ⓑ | 2 Ⓑ,Ⓒ | 3 Ⓐ | 4 Ⓐ |
| 5 Ⓓ | 6 Ⓓ | 7 Ⓐ | 8 Ⓒ |

9 Fact: ②, ④ Not a Fact: ①, ③

| 10 Ⓑ | 11 Ⓒ | 12 Ⓒ | 13 Ⓐ |
| 14 Ⓓ | 15 Ⓑ | | |

16 Fact: ②, ③ Not a Fact: ①, ④   17 Ⓑ

Scripts & Explanations

PART 1 Conversation 🎧 07-01   p.119

M Student Housing Office Employee: Good morning. Is there something I can do for you?

W Student: Good morning. Yes, I sure hope there is. I have a problem with my dorm room.

M: Then you've come to the right place. What's wrong with it?

W: The window is broken.

M: How did you do that?

W: I didn't do anything. I just got back from winter break about thirty minutes ago. When I went into my room, the first thing I noticed was that it was freezing. As I looked around the room to try to determine the problem, I saw that the window had a huge crack in it, so it was letting cold air from outside in.

M: Oh, I'm really sorry to hear that. Where do you live?

W: I live on the third floor of Crawford Hall.

M: Oh . . . I know what the problem is.

W: What?

M: As you know, sometimes dorm rooms are used by other people during summer and winter breaks. Crawford Hall was used by a group of students who were taking intensive classes here.

W: Yeah, I had to put all of the stuff in my room in storage before I went home for winter break. So I knew someone was staying in the room, but I didn't know who.

M: Apparently, some of the students who were living were a bit, uh, rowdy. The residential assistants working there were constantly reporting problems that they caused. I'm going to assume that your window was one of them.

W: But . . . shouldn't someone have checked each room when those students left? I mean, um, it's kind of irresponsible on the school's part not to have noticed and fixed the window before I got back. What happened?

M: Regretfully, a mistake happened. I'm really sorry about this problem.

W: That's fine, but what are you going to do about it? I need to get all of my possessions out of storage and moved back into my room. I've also got my first class of the semester tomorrow morning. But there's no way I can stay in the room as it is. It's freezing. I'll catch a cold at best if I stay there tonight.

M: You're absolutely right. Unfortunately, there's no way we can get a window repairman to your room today. Tomorrow afternoon is the best we can do.

W: So . . . what am I supposed to do in the meantime?

M: First, we're going to put you up in a hotel for the night. The school has plans for incidents like this, so you'll be staying at the Bayside Hotel, which is just down the street from the school. The cost of the room will be covered by the school, and so will any transportation fees you incur getting there and back.

W: Great. And what about my stuff?

M: I'll make sure that someone brings everything you have in storage up to your room for you no later than tomorrow morning. Now, uh, I just need you to fill out a couple of forms so that we can get this process started. I also need to see your student ID card.

W: Of course. Thanks for helping me get this matter settled.

1 Gist-Content Question

Ⓑ According to the student, her room is too cold because of a broken window, so she cannot stay in it.

2 Understanding Function Question

Ⓐ The man explains the reason that the student has a problem when he tells her about the intensive classes during winter break.

3 Detail Question

Ⓒ, Ⓓ First, the man says, "Unfortunately, there's no way we can get a window repairman to your room today. Tomorrow afternoon is the best we can do." Then, he adds, "First, we're going to put you up in a hotel for the night. The school has plans for incidents like this, so you'll be staying at the Bayside Hotel, which is just down the street from the school."

4 Detail Question

Ⓐ The man tells the student, "Now, uh, I just need you to fill out a couple of forms so that we can get this process started."

5 Understanding Attitude Question

Ⓓ During the conversation, the man is very sympathetic to and understanding of the student's situation and does his best to help her.

PART 1 Lecture 🎧 07-02   p.122

M Professor: Something you need to be aware of is that deserts are not necessarily hot and sandy like the Sahara Desert. In fact, there are cold deserts, such as the Gobi, and Antarctica is even considered a desert. What makes an area of land a desert is that it gets a minimal amount of precipitation each year. Most experts say that a region which gets fifty centimeters of precipitation or fewer a year is a desert. However, please keep this next point in mind: There is water in deserts. That's what I would like to talk about now.

Most people assume that deserts are barren lands, and that's true for the most part. But most of you are going to be surprised by what I tell you right now. It's actually possible to find water in deserts in many places. Now, uh, I'm not referring to the water that fills wadis and causes flooding when deserts get rain. I'm talking about water which can be found throughout the entire year. Yes, Betthany?

W Student: The Nile River is one example of water in the desert. I went on a cruise down the Nile with my family a couple of years ago, and we saw nothing but desert except around the banks of the river.

M: That was actually the first thing I was planning to talk about. There are some rivers that flow through deserts. Again, I'm not referring to temporary rivers that appear after rainstorms. The Nile River, which flows through the Sahara Desert in Africa, is the longest of these rivers. It's not the only one though. The Colorado River in the

United States flows through three different deserts. They are the Great Basin, the Sonoran, and the Mojave deserts.

Those are the two rivers which most people know about, but there are a few others. An interesting one is the Amargosa River. It flows for almost 290 kilometers through the Mojave Desert and also goes into Death Valley. The most interesting thing about the Amargosa River is that it only flows on the surface in a few places. Most of the time, this river flows underneath the surface. And that's where most of the water that exists in the desert can be found.

Ah, but I'm getting ahead of myself. Before I get into underground water sources, I need to talk about one more type of water that can be found aboveground. Betthany, you were in Egypt, so you must have seen one or two of these. Do you know what I'm talking about?

W: Oases, sir. My family went to one, but I don't recall the name. It was incredible to see what was, uh, essentially a big lake with lots of trees growing around it in the middle of the desert.

M: Well done, Betthany. An oasis, class, is an area where fresh water can be found in a dry or semidry area such as a desert. In most cases, oases occur where underground water bubbles up to the surface of the land. Oases are some of the most important places in deserts as nomads and other travelers use them to replenish their water supplies and to provide water for their camels and other animals when they are traveling through the desert. Some are very small, like, uh, a well. Others, such as the Al-Ahsa Oasis on the Arabian Peninsula, can be enormous. The Al-Ahsa Oasis is the world's largest one, covers more than eighty-five square kilometers, and provides water for both people and farms in the region.

The locations of oases are well known to desert travelers. For instance, the Sahara Desert has more than ninety oases, almost all of which have saved the lives of thirsty travelers at times. This water in the Sahara comes from an enormous aquifer that exists beneath the desert. In case you don't know, an aquifer is an underground layer of rock which contains groundwater. In some places, the water in that aquifer seeps to the surface and forms oases. The Sahara isn't the only desert with aquifers as they can be found pretty much everywhere. If you dig deep enough in some places, you'll get water.

And that brings us to another source of water in deserts: wells. Yes, it's possible to dig a well in a desert and to get water so long as you dig in the right spot. In fact, people have been digging wells in deserts for thousands of years. Like oases, the locations of these wells were, uh, well known to the denizens of deserts. They consider it their responsibility to take care of these wells so that others could use the water found in them. These wells sustained both people and animals. Today, thanks to modern technology, it's possible to dig deep wells in deserts to gain access to water that has certainly been underneath the ground for thousands of years.

6 Gist-Content Question

Ⓑ The professor mainly talks about sources of water in deserts in his lecture.

7 Understanding Organization Question

Ⓐ The professor comments, "The most interesting thing about the Amargosa River is that it only flows on the surface in a few places. Most of the time, this river flows underneath the surface."

8 Detail Question

Ⓐ, Ⓓ About oases, the professor remarks, "Other travelers use them to replenish their water supplies and to provide water for their camels and other animals when they are traveling through the desert." Then, he adds, "The Al-Ahsa Oasis is the world's largest one, covers more than eighty-five square kilometers, and provides water for both people and farms in the region."

9 Making Inferences Question

Ⓓ In stating, "The Al-Ahsa Oasis is the world's largest one, covers more than eighty-five square kilometers, and provides water for both people and farms in the region," the professor implies that agriculture is practiced around the Al-Ahsa Oasis.

10 Gist-Purpose Question

Ⓑ The professor comments, "In case you don't know, an aquifer is an underground layer of rock which contains groundwater. In some places, the water in that aquifer seeps to the surface and forms oases."

11 Connecting Content Question

Oases: ②   Wells: ①, ③, ④

About oases, the professor notes, "In most cases, oases occur where underground water bubbles up to the surface of the land." As for wells, the professor notes, "Like oases, the locations of these wells were, uh, well known to the denizens of deserts. They consider it their responsibility to take care of these wells so that others could use the water found in them. These wells sustained both people and animals. Today, thanks to modern technology, it's possible to dig deep wells in deserts to gain access to water that has certainly been underneath the ground for thousands of years."

PART 2 Conversation 🎧 07-03   p.125

W Student: Excuse me, Professor Olson. I, uh, I know you don't have office hours scheduled until tomorrow, but, um, do you think you could answer a question or two, please? They're about the astronomy class you just taught yesterday.

M Professor: Sure. Please come in, um . . . I'm sorry, but I don't know your name. As you know, the class has more than 200 students, and we haven't had any assignments yet, so I simply don't know almost anyone's name. I do, however, recognize you. You always sit in the front row near the window.

W: Thank you for remembering, sir. My name is Laurie McCartney, and I'm a freshman. I'm thinking about majoring in Astronomy. I really love the class, but today's lesson was a bit, uh, confusing to me.

M: What exactly was confusing about it?

W: There was that one word you mentioned. Uh, the one without any vowels in it. It begins with an s . . .

M: Syzygy?

W: Yes, that's it. I'm really sorry, but do you think you could explain it to me again? [5] **It has something to do with eclipses, right? If I remember correctly, it's some kind of an eclipse, like a solar or lunar one.**

M: **I'm afraid that, uh, while you're partially correct, you're mostly incorrect.**

W: **And that's why I came here to you.** I just don't get it.

M: Okay. A syzygy happens when three celestial bodies are roughly in alignment with one another. For instance, let's say that the sun, the moon, and Earth are all lined up together. That's a syzygy.

W: Right. Wouldn't that also create an eclipse? But you said a syzygy isn't an eclipse. That's why I am confused.

M: Well . . . one possible result of a syzygy is an eclipse. That would definitely happen when Earth, the moon, and the sun are lined up. However, a syzygy doesn't always create an eclipse.

W: Could you give me an example, please?

M: Sure. Have you ever heard someone say that one of the planets—let's take Jupiter as an example—is in conjunction with Earth?

W: Yes, I've heard that many times. Oh . . . Is that a syzygy?

M: It sure is because it means that Earth, Jupiter, and the sun are approximately in a straight line. But there won't be an eclipse from that. The distances are just too great.

W: What about stars?

M: No, that can't happen because a syzygy can only take place within a gravitational system. In our case, that means the solar system. So basically, when three or more celestial objects are in alignment, that creates a syzygy.

W: Hmm . . . Something like that must happen a lot, especially for planets like Jupiter and Saturn, which have dozens and dozens of moons.

M: Very good, Laurie. I'm glad to see you comprehend the idea now. There's a bit more to the concept, such as how a syzygy can result in what is called a transit or an occultation, but I'm afraid I've got to make an important call right now. So we'll need to have that talk another time.

W: No worries at all, sir. I believe I understand what a syzygy is enough now. I'll do some more reading, and if I have any questions, I'll visit during your office hours. Thank you.

M: Wonderful. Thanks for coming.

1 Gist-Content Question

Ⓑ The student and the professor mostly talk about a term—syzygy—that the professor discussed in class.

2 Detail Question

Ⓑ, Ⓒ The professor says, "A syzygy happens when three celestial bodies are roughly in alignment with one another. For instance, let's say that the sun, the moon, and Earth are all lined up together. That's a syzygy." Then, the professor adds, "One possible result of a syzygy is an eclipse."

3 Understanding Attitude Question

Ⓐ The professor comments, "I'm glad to see you comprehend the idea now."

4 Making Inferences Question

Ⓐ The professor remarks, "I'm afraid I've got to make an important call right now. So we'll need to have that talk another time."

5 Understanding Function Question

Ⓓ First, the student provides an incorrect explanation of a syzygy. When the professor mentions that she is mostly incorrect, she remarks, "And that's why I came here to see you." It can therefore be inferred that she is confused about a matter.

PART 2 Lecture #1 🎧 07-04   p.128

W Professor: All right, uh, I'd like to move on to one of my personal favorite styles of architecture. Let me show you a few pictures on the screen first . . . Here is one . . . and another . . . and another . . . Notice the shape of the roof on this building . . . and this one . . . Take a look at the timber here . . . and see how decorative it is . . . Very nice, isn't it?

This is the style known as Tudor Architecture. It comes from England, and it's generally accepted that this school of architecture began in 1458 and ended in 1603. This was the period when the Tudor monarchs ruled the land. The monarchs were Henry VII, Henry VIII, Edward VI, Mary I, and Elizabeth I. Yes, you have a question?

M Student: Wait a minute. [11] My grandparents live in a house that looks just like one you showed, but, um . . . they live an hour away from here, not in England. What's up with that?

W: **Why don't you wait a bit, and then you'll understand?** Okay?

M: Sure. That's fine.

W: Excellent. Thanks. Now before I start describing Tudor Architecture in detail, I need to provide some historical context first. Tudor Architecture began in 1485, which was at the tail end of the Middle Ages in England. England at that time was in the process of moving into the Early Modern Period, so this was a time when there were political, cultural, and social changes. What happened back then was that rich landowners started experimenting when building homes. They used both new building methods and materials. These facts allowed houses to be constructed in a more decorative manner. In addition, the Tudor monarchs, particularly Henry VII and Henry VIII, were eager to show their power and wealth. They therefore commissioned the construction of palaces, homes, and churches around the country. They wanted grand, memorable buildings, so a new style was created.

One other factor I should mention is that the economy in England was improving then. Remember that the New World had been discovered in 1492, just a few years after the first Tudor monarch took the throne. England was engaging in trade during this period and was sending ships across the Atlantic. The country was becoming wealthier, and a prosperous middle class was emerging, too. These individuals were proud of their wealth and wanted to show it off, so they constructed large, elaborate homes. England was essentially a country on the rise, so this was an ideal time for a new type of architecture to emerge.

What about the features of Tudor Architecture? Let me focus on the exterior. Take a look at the roofs here . . . and here . . . and here . . . Notice how steep they are and the fact that they have multiple gables. Ah, the gables are the vertical triangular ends at the top here . . . and here . . . You should also observe that the gables are of varying sizes. That's especially noticeable in this house . . . The extremely steep pitch of the roof really makes the building stand out, doesn't it? Another benefit of roofs like this is that both rain and snow were able easily to fall to the ground after hitting the roof.

Now look here . . . Do you see the half-timbered façades on this building.

M: Half-timbered? I've never heard that expression before.

W: Ah, it means that the internal and external walls are constructed with a wood frame. Notice all the wood you can see here . . . Then, uh, the spaces between the timber are built with another type of material, such as plaster, brick, stone, or stucco. The result is that a decorative pattern is created. Geometric designs such as this . . . and this . . . were particularly popular during this period. There's a really nice contrast created by the dark wood and the lighter materials that fill the spaces in between. This is perhaps the easiest way to identify Tudor Architecture.

A couple other exterior features of Tudor Architecture are construction with red bricks . . . Bricks were often placed around windows, chimneys, and doors. Speaking of doors, the front doors were typically located off-center. And the windows tended to be long and rectangular in shape. Some windows in Tudor homes even featured stained glass. Here's one . . .

Now, uh, I want to show you some of the most famous examples of Tudor architecture, but first, I'd like to respond to the question asked earlier. As I stated, the Tudor Period ended in 1603, but there are homes built in the Tudor style here in this country. Well, in the 1800s, there was a renewal of interest in Tudor Architecture, and that led to the period called Tudor Revival. Homes, churches, and even some buildings on university campuses were constructed in the Tudor style. You can still see many Tudor homes here in the New England area, and if you visit cities such as New York, Chicago, and Detroit, you can tour neighborhoods that were heavily influenced by this period. I'll show some pictures of them soon, but let's return to England for now.

6 Gist-Content Question

(D) The professor mainly talks about the characteristics of Tudor Architecture in her lecture.

7 Understanding Attitude Question

(A) The professor states, "All right, uh, I'd like to move on to one of my personal favorite styles of architecture," and then begins to talk about Tudor Architecture.

8 Understanding Organization Question

ⓒ During the lecture, the professor shows pictures to the students and discusses various aspects of them.

9 Detail Question

Fact: 2, 4   Not a Fact: 1, 3

About Tudor Architecture, the professor notes, "Take a look at the roofs here . . . and here . . . and here . . . Notice how steep they are," and adds, "Ah, it means that the internal and external walls are constructed with a wood frame." However, she notes that the homes are made of many different materials and are not made entirely with wood. She also points out, "Speaking of doors, the front doors were typically located off-center," so the homes do not have entrances in their exact centers.

10 Making Inferences Question

Ⓑ At the end of the lecture, the professor states, "I'll show some pictures of them soon, but let's return to England for now."

11 Understanding Function Question

ⓒ When the professor suggests that the student wait a bit for an answer, the professor implies that she will answer his question later in the lecture.

PART 2 Lecture #2 🎧 07-05   p.131

W Professor: Space telescopes are among the most important tools for astronomers. As they're located in orbit around Earth, they don't have to deal with blurring caused by the planet's atmosphere, which is a problem that ground-based telescopes must endure. There have been quite a few space telescopes launched. Since we've been discussing exoplanets today, I'd like to focus on the telescope that has been the most vital in that regard. I'm referring to the Kepler Space Telescope, which has been responsible for the discovery of thousands of exoplanets.

Let me give you some background about the telescope first. The primary person responsible for the Kepler was William Borucki, a NASA scientist. He had advocated for a space telescope that would search for exoplanets since the 1980s. However, his requests were constantly rejected, uh, mainly due to the fact that the technology necessary didn't exist. [17] Well, finally, it did exist, and in 2001, the 600-million-dollar project was finally approved. Kepler launched in 2009 and was expected to be functional for a year. **Let me say that it greatly exceeded expectations.**

M Student: In what way?

W: It wasn't retired until 2018, when it finally ran out of fuel, so it lasted a total of nine years. During that time, it observed five hundred thousand stars and discovered more than 2,600 planets. I should add that there are thousands of other candidate planets which it also discovered. By that, I mean that astronomers believe they have discovered planets, yet they have not been able to confirm their beliefs yet. I'd say that's pretty successful, wouldn't you?

Interestingly, the vast majority of the planets discovered were in the constellation Cygnus. Everyone, hold out your hand as far as you can extend it . . . Look at your palm . . . That's about the amount of space Cygnus takes up in the night sky. So as you can see, Kepler was focused on a tiny area of space, yet it still managed to observe half a million stars. It was able to do that because its cameras were extremely sensitive.

M: But how did it see planets? I mean, some of those stars must have been thousands of light years away. There's no way Kepler could have actually observed any planets orbiting those stars.

W: You're absolutely right, Tim. Remember that we studied Johannes Kepler earlier this semester? Do any of you remember Kepler's Third Law . . . ? No . . . ? Okay, well, it states that if the length of a planet's year and the mass of the star it orbits are known, its average distance from the star can be calculated. Why is this important? Well, Kepler was able to measure the brightness of a star to a fraction of a percent. So it was basically looking for the dimming of a star's light, which would be caused by a planet moving in front of that star. In our solar system, Jupiter is the biggest planet and can block around one percent of the sun's light. Earth, which is much smaller, blocks less than 0.01 percent of the sun's light. So when we see that a star's light is being blocked, we know an exoplanet is doing it. When we know how much light is being blocked and how often it is being blocked, we can determine the size of the exoplanet as well as its orbital period.

Now, uh, let me stress that before Kepler, most exoplanets discovered were gas giants. At that time, astronomers believed that there were few rocky planets in the universe and that gas giants dominated. Well . . . we were wrong. Most of the planets Kepler discovered are roughly between the sizes of Earth and Neptune. Neptune, by the way, is around four times the size of our planet. Most of those exoplanets are rocky planets, which is something we simply were not expecting. Another important discovery by Kepler is that virtually every star in the galaxy has at least one planet orbiting it. Many astronomers previously believed planets were rare, but that's far from true. There are more planets than stars in the galaxy, and that means there are countless worlds to explore . . . sometime in the future if we ever gain the capability to engage in interstellar travel.

Some of the things that Kepler discovered were simply incredible. For instance, some exoplanets orbit double stars. In some star systems, there are multiple planets orbiting as close as Mercury orbits our sun. Here's an interesting planet it discovered. Kepler-62e is a super-Earth, meaning it has a mass larger than our planet, and it is believed to be a water world. Kepler-62f is another possible water world. They both most likely have global oceans. As we believe life originated in the oceans here, it's possible there could be extraterrestrial life on either of those planets, too. Here's another one . . .

12 Gist-Content Question

ⓒ The professor mainly lectures on the various discoveries made by the Kepler Space Telescope.

13 Detail Question

Ⓐ The professor states, "The primary person responsible for the Kepler was William Borucki, a NASA scientist. He had advocated for a space telescope that would search for exoplanets since the 1980s."

14 Understanding Function Question

Ⓓ The professor tells the students, "Everyone, hold out your hand as far as you can extend it . . . Look at your palm . . . That's about the amount of space Cygnus takes up in the night sky. So as you can see, Kepler was focused on a tiny area of space."

15 Understanding Organization Question

Ⓑ The professor uses Kepler's Third Law to explain how the Kepler Space Telescope located exoplanets by saying, "Okay, well, it states that if the length of a planet's year and the mass of the star it orbits are known, its average distance from the star can be calculated. Why is this important? Well, Kepler was able to measure the brightness of a star to a fraction of a percent. So it was basically looking for the dimming of a star's light, which would be caused by a planet moving in front of that star."

16 Detail Question

Fact: ②, ③ Not a Fact: ①, ④

About the Kepler Space Telescope, the professor states, "At that time, astronomers believed that there were few rocky planets in the universe and that gas giants dominated. Well . . . we were wrong. Most of the planets Kepler discovered are roughly between the sizes of Earth and Neptune. Neptune, by the way, is around four times the size of our planet. Most of those exoplanets are rocky planets, which is something we simply were not expecting. Another important discovery by Kepler is that virtually every star in the galaxy has at least one planet orbiting it." However, Kepler only found thousands of planets, not half a million of them. Kepler also operated from 2009 to 2018, so it was not in operation for more than two decades.

17 Understanding Attitude Question

Ⓑ When the professor remarks that Kepler "greatly exceeded expectations," she means that Kepler performed better than it was supposed to.

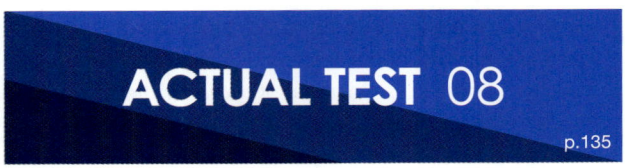

Answers

PART 1

1 Ⓓ	2 ⓒ	3 Ⓐ	4 Ⓑ
5 ⓒ	6 Ⓓ	7 Ⓓ	8 Ⓑ
9 ⓒ	10 Ⓑ	11 ⓒ	12 Ⓐ
13 Ⓓ	14 Ⓐ	15 Ⓑ	16 ⓒ

17 Fact: ①, ③ Not a Fact: ②, ④

PART 2

| 1 Ⓓ | 2 ⓒ, Ⓓ | 3 Ⓑ | 4 Ⓓ |
| 5 Ⓑ | 6 Ⓐ | 7 Ⓓ | 8 ⓒ |

9 Ganymede: ③, ④ Io: ① Europa: ②

10 Ⓑ 11 ⓒ

Scripts & Explanations

PART 1 Conversation 🎧 08-01 p.137

W Student: Hello, Professor Sellers. I'm here for our appointment.

M Professor: Good afternoon, Katherine. Thank you for coming on time. I really appreciate when students do that. It's much rarer than you would think. Please have a seat over there.

W: Yes, sir . . . So, um, what would you like to talk about with me today? I'm not in any kind of trouble, am I? I mean, uh, I thought I did pretty well on my midterm exams last week, but perhaps I messed up on one. Oh, no. You didn't get a call from the dean about me, did you?

M: It's nothing like that. I haven't gotten any reports on you from your current professors or from the dean, so I assume you did all right on your exams. I need to speak with you about an entirely different matter.

W: That's a relief.

M: Yes, I imagine that getting a poor grade on a midterm exam would be rather stressful. But that's not something you need to worry about today. Instead, I would like to talk to you about your future.

W: My . . . my future?

M: Yes, that's right. Basically, the school asks all academic advisors to speak with their students about their plans for the future. You know, after college.

W: But . . . but . . . I'm just a sophomore. I won't graduate for more than two years.

M: It's never too early to think about the future.

W: What do you mean?

M: Well, let me see . . . Many students study abroad during their junior year. This can be a great opportunity for students who are interested in learning a foreign language. But for those who have no interest in becoming bilingual or don't feel a need to learn about a foreign culture, there's no reason for them to study abroad.

W: Ah, I get what you're saying. If I think that living in Germany, Italy, or somewhere else may help me in my career after college, then I might want to give serious consideration to studying abroad.

M: Precisely. So . . . have you given any thought to your future?

W: Hmm . . . I can't really say that I have thought much about it. I guess I always kind of figured that I would go to graduate school after I finished my studies here.

M: And what would you prefer to study at graduate school? Do you want to continue your studies in economics?

W: I'm not really sure. I might get an MBA, but I might also attend law school instead.

M: Okay. What about getting a job right out of college? Have you thought about that?

W: Yes, I have, and I know that would be incredibly easy to do.

M: Easy? Why do you say that?

W: My father has his own company. He employs more than 250 people, and he has always told me that if I want to work there, he would hire me. However, he said I would have to start out in a low position and then work hard to earn a position in management.

M: Your father sounds like a smart man. It's much better to do that than to give you an upper-level position simply because you're the owner's daughter.

1 Gist-Purpose Question

(D) The professor tells the student, "I would like to talk to you about your future."

2 Making Inferences Question

(C) When the professor says, "Basically, the school asks all academic advisors to speak with their students about their plans for the future," it can be inferred that he is the student's academic advisor.

3 Detail Question

(A) When the professor says, "Many students study abroad during their junior year. This can be a great opportunity for students who are interested in learning a foreign language. But for those who have no interest in becoming bilingual or don't feel a need to learn about a foreign culture, there's no reason for them to study abroad," he is explaining what inspires some students to study in another country.

4 Making Inferences Question

(B) When the professor says, "Do you want to continue your studies in economics?" he is implying that the student is majoring in Economics.

5 Understanding Attitude Question

(C) The professor shows that he likes the way the student's father thinks when he says, "Your father sounds like a smart man. It's much better to do that than to give you an upper-level position simply because you're the owner's daughter."

PART 1 Lecture #1   08-02   p.140

M Professor: Ecosystem recovery is a term lots of people use nowadays. Many people discuss how humans are harming ecosystems and even causing them to collapse at times. They then mention the need for humans to help ecosystems recover. I think it's admirable that people want to help the environment improve, but it's not actually necessary. You see, uh, in most cases, ecosystems are capable of recovering by themselves. Sure, it might take years or even decades, but after some time, ecosystems often look mostly like they did before a disaster or calamity struck.

W Student: I remember the big forest fire here a decade ago. The entire area was blackened. Today, the forest looks incredible, and there are absolutely no signs of the fire anywhere. Is that what you're talking about?

M: Totally. Wildfires are a perfect example of how ecosystem recovery occurs. I'm planning on talking about them today. But first, I'd like to discuss a different type of natural disaster. We all know volcanoes can have devastating effects on the land. For instance, everyone is familiar with the story of Pompeii and how the volcano Vesuvius literally buried that city and its inhabitants. Well, what most people don't know is that volcanoes are constantly erupting around the world. ¹¹ Can anyone tell me how many volcanoes are currently erupting? Susan?

W: Um . . . five?

M: Not even close. I just checked before class started, and the answer is thirty-seven. Now, uh, some eruptions are minor ones. You know, just a bit of ash and smoke are coming out. Others are bigger with plenty of lava being expelled. In nearly every case, however, these volcanoes are causing destruction to their local ecosystems. You've probably seen videos of eruptions in, uh, Hawaii and Iceland. You can see lava pouring out around barren landscapes, especially in Iceland. Well, when volcanoes are continually erupting, it's hard for the land to recover. Yet some volcanoes may only erupt once every century or two. If you look at pictures of them today, they're surrounded by trees and other vegetation. How did they manage to recover . . . ? Let's find out.

The first thing we should consider is the type of eruption. For example, is the eruption one involving the spewing of ash or lava? If it's ash, the recovery will be much quicker. If it's lava, it could take centuries for the land to recover if the eruption happens on a large scale. Another important factor is access to water. Places that have lots of water or that are located in the tropics will recover much faster than places where water is less abundant.

We can begin with something fairly simple. Let's imagine that a volcano erupts and mostly spews out ash. Even if it's a thick layer, over time, the ash will mix with the soil, get washed away by water, or get blown away by the wind. There will be some places affected by the eruption where plants such as ferns start growing. Once that happens, the land becomes more fertile. Birds flying overhead may drop seeds, which results in other types of plants growing. In a relatively short period of time—by that, I mean just a few years—trees will be growing in some areas. These types of eruptions are fairly simple for ecosystems to recover from.

What about more powerful eruptions involving lava? Well, in 1959, Kīlauea Iki, a volcano in Hawaii, began erupting by spewing out fountains of lava several hundred meters in the sky. Of course, the devastation was great, but scientists were excited. Once the eruptions stopped, a couple of scientists visited some places affected by the eruption and marked off square plots of land. For the next four years, they continually returned to see how the land was recovering. They also went back seven and nine years later so that they could monitor the situation.

Those scientists learned that alga was the first organism to return to the area covered by lava. Next came lichens. Interestingly, in some places, both ferns and mosses appeared at the same time as lichens. This didn't happen overnight though. It was an extremely slow process. In year nine of the study, there were still few plants growing in most places. In fact, the land looked extremely barren. But today, it's a popular hiking place. There are still dead zones, but trees are growing in places now. There are cracks in the lava thanks mainly to rainwater, and that has enabled plants to get into those cracks and to start growing, which helps break down the lava. It's a slow process. After all, that eruption happened more than sixty years ago, but you can't expect quick recoveries in nature.

Of course, those can happen in some instances, even after powerful eruptions. Let me tell you about the recovery of the ecosystem around Mt. St. Helens. It was a volcano in the U.S. that blew its top in 1980 and devastated the area around it.

6 Gist-Content Question

   Ⓓ The professor mainly focuses on ecosystem recovery after volcanic eruptions in his lecture.

7 Understanding Organization Question

   Ⓓ The professor comments, "We all know volcanoes can have devastating effects on the land. For instance, everyone is familiar with the story of Pompeii and how the volcano Vesuvius literally buried that city and its inhabitants."

8 Detail Question

   Ⓑ About birds, the professor notes, "Birds flying overhead may drop seeds, which results in other types of plants growing."

9 Detail Question

   Ⓒ About Kīlauea Iki, the professor comments, "Those scientists learned that alga was the first organism to return to the area covered by lava."

10 Connecting Content Question

   Ⓑ First, the professor states, "Well, in 1959, Kīlauea Iki, a volcano in Hawaii, began erupting by spewing out fountains of lava several hundred meters in the sky. Of course, the devastation was great." Then, about Mt. St. Helens, the professor remarks, "Let me tell you about the recovery of the ecosystem around Mt. St. Helens. It was a volcano in the U.S. that blew its top in 1980 and devastated the area around it."

11 Understanding Attitude Question

Ⓒ When the professor tells the student, "Not even close," he means that the student's answer is far from correct.

PART 1 Lecture #2 🎧 08-03   p.143

W Professor: Chimpanzees are omnivores, and when given a choice, they prefer to eat fruits, nuts, and berries while also consuming plant leaves and seeds. These plant-based foods comprise the majority of their diet. Please be aware that the specific types of foods they consume depend on the individual species and their location though. Ripe fruit is one of their favorites, and chimpanzees especially love to eat figs, which are high in both sugar and fiber. Chimps in the wild have also been observed eating honey, insects, small birds, and small mammals. They have additionally been seen using tools when they hunt for insects and animals.

M Student: How much of their diet is based on insects and other animals?

W: Well, it really depends on the following: the species, the location of the troop, and the availability of other foods, particularly fruit and leaves. For the most part, however, it's safe to say that more than ninety percent of their diet is plant based, and in some places, up to ninety-eight percent is plant based. Still, chimps' behavior while they are hunting has attracted a great amount of interest when zoologists observe them in the wild. Their use of tools additionally shows their level of intelligence and problem-solving abilities.

The tools that chimps use are primarily sticks and rocks. For example, a chimp may sharpen a short stick with its teeth and then use the stick to penetrate a beehive for honey or an ant nest instead. One insect that chimps enjoy eating is the termite, which builds high dirt mounds for homes. Chimps use sharpened sticks to dig into termite homes and drag out the inhabitants to eat. Female chimps have also been seen using sharp sticks to dig small mammals called bushbabies out of hiding places in tree cavities. Some zoologists have even seen chimps using rocks to crack open the hard outer shells of seeds and nuts to access the tasty parts inside.

When hunting, chimps favor small lizards, frogs, birds, and various small mammals. Yet they will hunt large animals when the opportunity presents itself. One animal that they appear to favor above all others is the red colobus monkey, which makes up more than ninety percent of the prey that some troops of chimps hunt. How often they hunt varies both from troop to troop and from year to year. Observations of various troops in Africa show a wide variety of hunting intensity in different years. One troop of more than fifty chimps was observed hunting and killing around 150 animals one year while the same troop only hunted and killed twenty animals another year. In some troops, chimps go on what experts call hunting binges. One troop was observed hunting thirty-eight times during a seventy-four-day period. During that time, the chimpanzees in the troop killed more than seventy red colobus monkeys. Zoologists believe this change in behavior may have had to do with rising red colobus monkey populations or the addition of aggressive male chimps that enjoyed hunting to the hunting party. However, as yet, they have no solid reasons for the change in hunting behavior.

When they hunt, chimps work in packs to maximize the chances of a successful hunt. Some packs are small whereas others may have more than thirty chimps. Typically, the majority of the hunters are males. Each chimp has a specific role to play in a hunt. Some drive the prey toward other chimps, which are waiting to ambush the prey, while other chimps act as blockers to prevent prey from escaping in another direction. Chimps often chase red colobus monkeys into treetops and drive them toward an area with fewer trees to lessen the chances of the monkeys leaping from tree to tree and then escaping. When the prey is finally cornered and exhausted, the largest male chimp will attack and kill it by using its teeth. Then, the other chimps gather around to wait for a share of the meat. Normally, all of the chimps, uh, even those that didn't take part in the hunt, get to eat something. All of the meat is consumed, and the chimps even crack the bones open to get to the marrow inside them.

Something that zoologists have trouble determining is what time of the year chimps hunt. They have made general studies showing that the hunting activity of some troops increases during the dry season in Africa. Uh, that usually takes place in the summer. This may correspond with the lack of fruit and other plant-based food sources. Yet not all chimp troops behave in a similar manner, and some troops actually hunt more often during the rainy season, which is when fruits and plants are more readily available. So there are still many things that we just don't know about the hunting behavior of chimpanzees.

12 Gist-Content Question

Ⓐ The professor mainly discusses the eating and hunting habits of chimpanzees in her lecture.

13 Making Inferences Question

Ⓓ The professor states, "For the most part, however, it's safe to say that more than ninety percent of their diet is plant based, and in some places, up to ninety-eight percent is plant based." It can therefore be inferred that chimpanzees do not consume very much meat.

14 Understanding Attitude Question

Ⓐ The professor remarks, "Their use of tools additionally shows their level of intelligence and problem-solving abilities."

15 Understanding Organization Question

Ⓑ About the red colobus monkey, the professor points out, "One animal that they appear to favor above all others is the red colobus monkey, which makes up more than ninety percent of the prey that some troops of chimps hunt."

16 Making Inferences Question

Ⓒ The professor says, "When they hunt, chimps work in packs to maximize the chances of a successful hunt. Some packs are small whereas others may have more than thirty chimps." It can therefore be inferred that the number of members in the hunting packs varies.

17 Detail Question

Fact: 1, 3 Not a Fact: 2, 4

About chimpanzee hunting methods, the professor states, "Each chimp has a specific role to play in a hunt. Some drive the prey toward other chimps, which are waiting to ambush the prey, while other chimps act as blockers to prevent prey from escaping in another direction," and then adds, "When the prey is finally cornered and exhausted, the largest male chimp will attack and kill it by using teeth." However, it is not true that chimpanzees use weapons during their hunts, and the professor also adds, "Normally, all of the chimps, uh, even those that didn't take part in the hunt, get to eat something."

PART 2 Conversation 🎧 08-04   p.146

W Student: Oh, uh, before I go, there's one more thing I would like to chat with you about. I know you're busy today, but this shouldn't take too long.

M Professor: Sure. Go ahead.

W: I came up with a topic for my final paper, and I thought I would run it by you to get your approval first.

M: That sounds like a smart idea. What are you thinking of writing about?

W: I was hoping to write about the Spanish Armada. Uh, you know, the armada that was defeated by the British in 1588.

M: Yes, I'm familiar with it. What approach are you going to take when you write about it?

W: I thought I would mention how it was a completely unprovoked attack by the Spanish on the British.

M: [4] Um . . . where did you hear that it was an unprovoked attack?

W: I can't remember. I think I read it somewhere on the Internet.

M: You know, it's not always best to believe everything you read online.

W: Why is that? Is there something wrong with what I just said?

M: There is. The attack by the Spanish was most certainly not unprovoked. In fact, relations between the Spanish and the British had been poor for at least a couple of decades.

W: Why was that?

M: There were two primary reasons. One was religion while the other had to do with Spain's colonies in the New World.

W: The colonies? What do you mean?

M: Remember how we discussed the fact that the Spanish regarded their New World colonies as opportunities to extract as much wealth as possible? The Spanish were focused on obtaining gold, silver, jewels, and other treasures in the New World and then transporting them across the Atlantic Ocean to enrich the coffers of Spain.

W: Yes, I remember that. What does that have to do with the Spanish Armada though?

M: Many British ships were basically privateers. They were therefore permitted by the British crown to prey upon Spanish treasure ships by attacking those ships. Essentially, uh, they were interested in plundering the loot that the Spanish were taking back to Europe. One of the most successful privateers, of course, was Sir Francis Drake, who, uh, as you should know . . .

W: He commanded the British forces that attacked the Spanish Armada.

M: Right you are. Now, uh, the other main point of contention between the Spanish and the British was religion. Spain was Catholic, but the British had abandoned Catholicism and turned to Protestantism. Philip II of Spain had long considered attacking and conquering the British and forcing them to return to the Catholic faith. Please remember that religion was a huge part of people's lives in the past, so this was of great importance to people on both sides.

W: [5] Hmm . . . It seems like what I read was wrong. I believe I need to reconsider what I'm planning to write.

M: **I'm glad you came to that conclusion.** I don't believe you should abandon the topic though. I think you just need to consider writing about a different aspect of it.

W: I will. Thanks. Let me think about it for a couple of days, and then I'll come back to chat with you the next time that you hold office hours.

1 Gist-Content Question

Ⓓ The student remarks, "I came up with a topic for my final paper, and I thought I would run it by you to get your approval first."

2 Detail Question

Ⓒ, Ⓓ First, the professor says, "Many British ships were basically privateers. They were therefore permitted by the British crown to prey upon Spanish treasure ships by attacking those ships. Essentially, uh, they were interested in plundering the loot that the Spanish were taking back to Europe." Then, he adds, "Now, uh, the other main point of contention between the Spanish and the British was religion. Spain was Catholic, but the British had abandoned Catholicism and turned to Protestantism. Philip II of Spain had long considered attacking and conquering the British and forcing them to return to the Catholic faith."

3 Understanding Organization Question

Ⓑ The professor notes, "One of the most successful privateers, of course, was Sir Francis Drake."

4 Understanding Function Question

Ⓓ When the professor says. "It's not always best to believe everything you read online," he is telling the student that she has some incorrect information.

5 Understanding Attitude Question

Ⓑ When the professor says, "I'm glad you came to that conclusion," he is agreeing with the student's decision to reconsider what she is planning to write.

PART 2 Lecture 🎧 08-05   p.149

M Professor: In 1610, Galileo Galilei took his relatively new invention, a telescope, and trained it on Jupiter. He immediately noticed four dots around the planet. Over time, he observed that these dots appeared to move, which enabled him to surmise that they were moons orbiting the planet. These moons, Io, Ganymede, Europa, and Callisto, are the four largest of Jupiter's moons and are collectively known as the Galilean moons.

W Student: Professor Wilcox, is it true that Jupiter has more than ninety moons? I heard it was somewhere around sixty just a couple of years ago.

M: Ah, at the present time, Jupiter is confirmed to have ninety-five moons, but that number is subject to change. You are correct that Jupiter was thought to have around sixty moons just a while ago, but as telescopes have improved and more people have trained their eyes on the outer planets, more and more moons are being discovered and confirmed. Saturn, for instance, was once thought to have fewer moons than Jupiter, but it has 146 confirmed moons right now. Both planets are bound to see those numbers increase in the future as well.

Now, uh, let me return to the Galilean moons. They are among the most fascinating in the solar system, each for a different reason. Let me go into detail on all four of them for you. I'm going to start with Ganymede, which is so large that if it didn't orbit Jupiter but instead orbited the sun, it would be considered a planet. In fact, Ganymede is the biggest moon in the solar system and is even larger than the planet Mercury. Ganymede is the only moon in the solar system to have its own magnetic field and is also covered with a thick layer of ice. Astronomers believe there may be various layers of oceans beneath that icy layer, so many speculate that Ganymede has more liquid water than any celestial body in the solar system, uh, including Earth.

W: Is it possible that life exists on Ganymede, you know, uh, like in its oceans?

M: Hmm . . . That's a good question. I suppose it's possible; however, the icy outer layer of Ganymede is around 150 kilometers thick, so I doubt we'll ever get down to the liquid water layers to learn if there is any life there. Uh, at least until we develop better technology than what exists today.

Let's move on to the second-largest of the Galilean moons and the third-biggest one in the solar system. This would be Callisto. Callisto is just slightly smaller than Mercury. Interestingly, Callisto is comprised of both rock and ice, but the two are not really separated, so it's sort of like a rocky ice ball. Its orbit is farther from Jupiter than the other Galilean moons, so it's less affected by Jupiter's gravity than the other three moons are. It's covered with impact craters and is believed to have a liquid ocean deep beneath its surface. Honestly, of the Galilean moons, it's the least interesting, so let's talk about the next one.

Io is the third-largest of the Galilean moons and is noted primarily for its volcanic activity. As a matter of fact, it has eruptions happening on its surface nearly all of the time. Astronomers have identified more than 400 active volcanoes on Io up to now. One reason this moon is so volcanically active is that it orbits Jupiter very close to the planet, so Jupiter's powerful gravity influences Io and contributes to the eruptions. One impact of all of these eruptions is that the surface of Io is constantly changing. Whereas Callisto is believed to have the oldest unaltered surface in the solar system, Io's is surely the newest because of the lava that flows over it and makes it undergo changes.

Now, let's get to the smallest of the four Galilean moons but what is, in my opinion, the most interesting one. I'm referring to Europa. Europa has an extremely smooth surface, which is almost surely being kept that way by liquid water beneath the outer layer of the moon. Space probes that examined Europa sent back data indicating that it has an absolutely enormous ocean around 100 kilometers deep that starts about thirty kilometers from the surface. This is where we believe that life, uh, if it exists elsewhere in the solar system, may be found. There are currently two space probes which will be examining Europa when they arrive at Jupiter, and it's likely that more will be sent in the future.

Okay, uh, I'd like to go on about Europa a bit more, but I believe it's time for a short break. Let's take a ten-minute break, and then we'll continue. If any of you haven't submitted your homework yet, please give it to me right now.

6 Gist-Content Question

Ⓐ The professor focuses on the primary characteristics of the Galilean moons in his lecture.

7 Making Inferences Question

Ⓓ In talking about Jupiter and Saturn, the professor remarks, "Both planets are bound to see those numbers increase in the future as well." He therefore implies that the number of moons both planets have will increase in the future.

8 Understanding Organization Question

Ⓒ The professor talks about the Galilean moons by starting with the largest and then moving to the smallest.

9 Connecting Content Question

Ganymede: ③, ④   Io: ①   Europa: ②

Regarding Ganymede, the professor states, "Ganymede is the only moon in the solar system to have its own magnetic field," and then adds, "The icy outer layer of Ganymede is around 150 kilometers thick." As for Io, the professor says, "Astronomers have identified more than 400 active volcanoes on Io up to now." About Europa, the professor remarks, "There are currently two space probes which will be examining Europa when they arrive at Jupiter."

10 Detail Question

Ⓑ The professor tells the students, "Europa has an extremely smooth surface, which is almost surely being kept that way by liquid water beneath the outer layer of the moon."

11 Making Inferences Question

Ⓒ At the end of the lecture, the professor says, "I believe it's time for a short break. Let's take a ten-minute break, and then we'll continue."

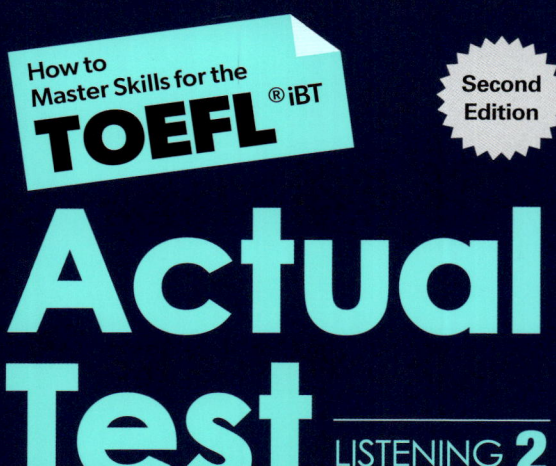